A Matter of Fact

Using Factual Texts in the Classroom

Pamela Green

ELEANOR CURTAIN
PUBLISHING

First published in 1992
ELEANOR CURTAIN PUBLISHING
906 Malvern Road
Armadale Vic 3143

Copyright © Pamela Green 1992

All rights reserved.
No part of this publication may
be reproduced in any form without
prior permission of the publisher.

National Library of Australia
Cataloguing-in-publication data:

Green, Pamela, 1958 —.
    A Matter of Fact: using factual texts
in the classroom.
    ISBN 1 875327 13 4.

    1. Research — study and teaching (Primary).
    2. Information science-study and teaching
    (Primary). 3. Reference books — Study and
    teaching (Primary). 4. Language arts
    (Primary). I. Title.
    372.130281

Produced by Sylvana Scannapiego,
Island Graphics
Edited by Ruth Siems
Text design by Sarn Potter
Cover design by David Constable
Cover photograph by Bill Thomas
Typeset in Baskerville/Futura
by Optima Typesetting and Design,
Melbourne
Printed in Australia by Impact Printers

CONTENTS

Acknowledgements	vi
Preface	vii
1 Towards a view of language learning	1
2 Getting to know factual texts	15
3 Starting off with factual texts: a glimpse from a Prep classroom	34
4 Taking up new challenges: a case study from a Year 2/3 classroom	58
5 Literacy demands in a Year 6 class	81
6 Classroom strategies	97
7 Getting started or expanding options	122
References	131
Index	135

ACKNOWLEDGEMENTS

The support from the following people while planning and writing this book must be acknowledged:

Elaine Furniss, whose initial encouragement inspired this book and whose informed critical comment was most appreciated along the way;

Michael Green, a great Prep teacher (and more), who shared much of his time, expertise and patience;

Andrea Johnson, an energetic and thoughtful colleague (and wonderful teacher), who welcomed me into her Year 6 class;

Darrel Caulley, whose expertise led me into the world of research;

Reg and Mon Billing, last but not least, who have been conferencing with me since I first put pen to paper.

PREFACE

This book is about language learning, the roles of teachers and children in reading and writing classrooms, and how factual texts can be incorporated into the primary school classroom. There are three case studies: Prep Year, Year 2/3 and Year 6.

A comment by one of my Year 3 children had lasting impact on my own writing, so much so that I decided to write this book. Luke commented, 'If you write a book, you don't just go and put it on a shelf and don't let no one read it. So you sit on a chair and read it to everybody.' So, when I completed a Master of Education based on research about reading and writing factual texts in my Year 2/3 classroom, I decided to do something with it.

It was not until I had been teaching for a few years and returned to study that I truly recognised the need for a theoretical framework. Without such a framework we do not know *why* we do what we do daily in our classrooms. Even if we know a fair amount about *how* to do things, without the *why* we lack credibility and accountability. The theory is not where I started in practice: my first year was fairly much a matter of survival, but from then on theory and practice became intertwined so that if someone asked why I taught in a certain way I could explain, providing more than an intuitive reply. Not that intuition is not part of teaching. It is. But on its own it is not convincing to a worried parent nor, if we are honest, to ourselves. So I begin with the theory because it really does help the practice stand up. You might find that it merely substantiates what you know or throws light on something new or goes against your view. I hope so. We need as much healthy discussion and debate as we can find.

The implications of this book will be most felt by teachers who themselves act as researchers and monitor the impact of such explicit teaching on their own practice and the ramifications for the classroom. As Jaggar (1989) stated '...no specific theory or research study or curriculum guide can prescribe what is appropriate for individual students in a particular classroom.' (p.74) The need for teachers to take up their own research is vital as teacher research seems to have the most impact on classroom practice. Existing instances of teacher research, such as that presented in this book, provide starting points or examples from which further teacher research may evolve.

Pam Green

1
TOWARDS A CRITICAL VIEW OF LANGUAGE LEARNING

♦

Momentous change has occurred in recent times in the understanding of how children learn language and our perceptions of how we, as teachers, can promote language learning. Much has been written about language learning but still the question persists. How can we effectively promote language learning in our classrooms? A brief look at some of the major moves in literacy education over the last two or three decades shows us where our theory stems from and provides a basis for considering future directions and implications for classroom practice.

THE SEVENTIES: A TIME OF CHANGE
EXPERIENCES BEFORE SCHOOL

The impact of Bernstein's theory of 'elaborated' and 'restricted' codes was felt by educators in the early 1970s. Bernstein's work increased awareness of the differences between children's experiences with language prior to schooling. He examined the language of young children from different 'classes' and found some children using 'restricted' codes while others used language codes that he termed 'elaborate' or complex. Bernstein's theory met with some initial criticism that it made working class children with 'restricted' language codes seem inferior. As a result, he modified his theory and stated that the 'restricted' language code that is generated in certain subcultures must not be seen as insignificant. (Bernstein 1971, p.199)

Bernstein's work highlighted the need to acknowledge the experiences and language competencies that children bring to school and to take into account the differences that may exist. Doubt was shed on the 'empty vessel' notion which depicted children arriving at school as empty vessels awaiting the transmission of knowledge by the teacher. This view of education as transmission began to diminish as educators realised the wealth of experience that young children brought to school.

LANGUAGE EXPERIENCE APPROACHES

Language experience was part of the child-centred view of education of the seventies. The effect of the work by early philosophers such as Rousseau was evident in these approaches. He emphasised the child as central in learning and described learning through play and through first-hand experiences.

Language experience approaches also drew on the work of Ashton-Warner (1963) who wrote about 'the bridge from the known to the unknown.' (p.26) Her organic approach to language learning recognised the experiences that children brought to school and used them as the 'bridge' or the link between home and school and a starting point for reading and writing.

With language experience approaches came a belief that children needed to exhibit positive attitudes towards reading and therefore required opportunities to read for real purposes. (Goddard 1974, p.23) Structured reading methods such as 'the phonic word method', which simplified the reading process, and those approaches which restricted material to published reading schemes were rejected.

The commercially produced kit *Breakthrough to Literacy* (1970), encouraged children to recount events that occurred at home while teachers transcribed the children's sentences onto sentence strips and cards which could then be manipulated on sentence boards. Language experience drew on children's oral language and made links with written language. The child as learner was central. As Pigdon and Woolley (1989) tell us 'there was a strong view that children should begin their more formal engagement with written language by writing, or having their own oral language written down for them.' (p.58) Writing in this approach was controlled largely by the teacher. There was little child ownership of writing.

Language experience approaches represented a major swing from traditional views of language learning. For example, the traditional view of the process of learning written language using phonic approaches could be represented as follows:

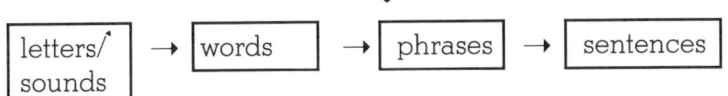

In simplistic terms, language experience approaches reversed the direction of the process, although in reality it is much more complex.

MOVING INTO THE EIGHTIES
PROCESS WRITING

The catch-phrase of the early eighties was 'process-writing' which came into the limelight when Donald Graves visited Australia in 1980. For a time the focus swung away from reading and onto writing. In process-writing classrooms children were encouraged to take responsibility for their writing and to write freely about what they knew best: their own experiences. Children worked as authors, engaging in stages of rehearsal, drafting and redrafting, conferencing and publishing.

The work of researchers such as Bissex (1980) and Bean and Bouffler (1987) were significant in encouraging teachers to trust young children's early explorations, including invented spelling, as a natural part of

How can we effectively promote language learning in our classrooms?

learning to write. This freed teachers from feeling compelled to act as scribe for young writers and enabled children to develop a sense of ownership over their writing.

The issue of when to intervene and insist on correct surface features, such as spelling, was hotly debated by parents, teachers and teacher educators. However, in many process-writing classrooms teachers who were concerned about child choice or who were perhaps unsure of their own role in the process avoided intervention and tended to take a back seat in their language teaching.

This child-centred approach focused on process rather than product, as indicated by the term 'process-writing' which is actually a tautology.

THE CONFERENCE APPROACH

There was concern in process-writing classrooms about opportunities for teachers and children to talk about their writing on a one-to-one basis or in small groups. The work of teacher-researchers such as Parry and Hornsby (1985) provided practical insights about organising writing workshops in primary classrooms. The conference was portrayed as the focal point of the writing process and suggestions were given to help teachers conduct a range of conferences or discussions at various stages of development of a piece of writing.

Walshe (1981) recognised that young children arriving at school were keen to write. He insisted that children could learn to write before formally learning to read, spell or use handwriting conventions. These ideas were not new. Walshe noted Montessori's research in the early 1920s, which found that preschool children who had learned the alphabet were writing words before learning to read, and the work of Steiner, who founded a number of schools in the mid-1920s in Germany. Steiner believed in allowing children to write before learning to read as many children learn to read through their own writing. Walshe saw the conference approach as founded on four 'pillars': ownership, conference, process and time. (Walshe 1981, pp.121-3) Conferencing with children about their writing recognised the importance of feedback and of having a real audience.

For a time, writing rather than reading was the focus. Gradually, however, the links between reading and writing were noted, although it was a long time before they were fully recognised. At the beginning of the 1970s, Britton (1970) described the influence of reading on writing: 'As the influence of the written language increases their [students'] progress in writing depends more and more on the nature of the reading input.' (p.38) At about the same time Chomsky (1972) showed the correlation between reading exposure and language development. Smith's (1983) term 'reading like a writer' alerted teachers and children to the value of searching for writing ideas when reading.

Published texts were seen to provide examples for writing. Similarly, the term 'writing like a reader' emerged as the importance of writers taking into account their audience (the reader) was acknowledged. 'Real' literature was emphasised.

Language workshops in both reading and writing occurred in many classrooms. Hornsby, Sukarna and Parry (1986) describe reading workshops and the conferences which were part of them. The conference approach to language learning grew, and had a marked impact on the way we taught as well as highlighting the importance of talking and listening in the reading and writing classroom.

WHOLE LANGUAGE APPROACHES

By the late seventies and early eighties, a move towards what have been termed holistic approaches to language learning emerged. Researchers such as Holdaway (1979) and Cambourne (1984) studied the ways in which children develop oral language. Research findings were transferred from oracy to literacy growth in the classroom. A number of significant case studies showed instances of language learning from the classroom. Teachers became 'kidwatchers' influenced by the work of Yetta Goodman (1978). The work of Calkins (1983), Butler and Turbill (1984), Hansen (1987), Atwell (1987) and Brown and Mathie (1990) showed the insights that could be gained from conducting research about literacy and learning from one's own classroom.

The links between reading and writing were further stressed. Calkins emphasised such links when she wrote, '...there was no way I could watch writing without watching reading.' (1983, p.153) The teacher's role was becoming clearer. Cambourne's seven conditions of learning — immersion, demonstration, expectation, responsibility, approximation, employment (practice) and feedback — were being considered when planning for the classroom. Cambourne later added another condition, engagement, to provide a more comprehensive view of language learning. (Cambourne 1988) Teaching strategies were also being investigated further. Hansen recommended that teachers organise the classroom to provide time, choice, response, structure and community in order to develop a community of readers and writers.

Whole language approaches emphasised the links between the four modes of language: listening, speaking, reading and writing. Ken Goodman (1986) stated that language is '...inclusive, and it is indivisible.' (p.27) He urged teachers to consider language in terms of whole texts: when looking at smaller units of language, such as words and phrases, we need to do so in the context of '...whole, real language texts that are part of real language experiences of children.' (p.28)

Unlike traditional approaches to language education, where little attention was given to content, whole language learning focused on process as well as content. Whole language teachers '...treat content seriously, not merely as entertainment or as glue to hold separate subjects together (e.g., writing about dinosaurs, doing arithmetic problems about dinosaurs, reading about dinosaurs, and so on.) But rarely does their inevitable shaping of the study include a nudge toward gender or race or class issues in relation to whatever the topic is. Rarely are children taught to ask: who benefits from this interpretation? from this fact? from asking this question?' (Edelsky 1991, pp.165-6) The need to consider content matter more critically and in terms of the cultural context became apparent.

THREE COMPONENTS OF LANGUAGE

Halliday's view of what happens when one learns language has contributed enormously to what we know about language learning and teaching. Language learning may be seen to involve three main components: '...learning language, learning through language and learning about language.' (Halliday 1981, p.7)

These components are '...so interrelated that in many practical instances it is difficult to separate them.' (Christie, 1985, p.30) For instance, when a child learns how to ask a caregiver for a drink and says, 'Drink,' the child is learning how to speak. At the same time, the child is learning how to use language to achieve a personal goal. Clearly the child is learning language, learning through language and learning about language but just where one aspect begins and ends is not easily distinguishable.

LANGUAGE LEARNING

Language learning occurs from birth. We continually refine the language we need as we work towards mastering oral and written language skills. The context dictates the purpose to which language is put, and the demands made upon the language user, and learning language that is appropriate to the context occurs through personal and social language use. This refinement of language is a continual lifetime process.

LEARNING THROUGH LANGUAGE

Language is vital to learning. Our thinking processes are inextricably linked to language. Through language we make sense of the world, make judgements about our experience and communicate with others.

LEARNING ABOUT LANGUAGE

As we use language, we learn which language is appropriate in particular contexts. Language is a system with elements, such as meaning and grammar, which are difficult to separate. How language is structured and used varies according to the cultural context.

Halliday's model lets us see 'where each facet enters into the overall growth and development of a child.' (Halliday 1981, p.7) As language users learn language, learn through language and learn about language, they gain control of language and are better able to participate in society. Language learning is an achievement that has both personal and social dimensions, and occurs within and beyond the classroom.

GENRE APPROACHES

Genre approaches to language emerged in the latter part of the 1980s. These are based on 'quality texts which show how writers express real world knowledge in a variety of genres [which provide] access to appropriate published models which children and teachers can use to extend their text repertoires.' (Pigdon & Woolley 1989, p.60) What is highlighted is the need to expose children to a broad range of quality texts, particularly factual texts.

WHOLE LANGUAGE vs GENRE

The debate between supporters of whole language approaches and those who favour genre approaches has been running for the last few years, but we can no longer afford to allow this debate to polarise our thinking and teaching. We need to seek connections, and reflect on how each approach might complement the other so that we can continue with the task at hand: teaching and learning more about the world we live in.

Whole language approaches and genre approaches should be seen as complementary. For instance, whole language approaches can be seen to emphasise language learning processes, while genre approaches can be seen to highlight products of language learning and teaching. We need to acknowledge both process and product so that our view of language learning is more comprehensive and more likely to meet our changing needs. We can do this, not by focusing on one approach at the expense of the other, but by putting the two together and learning from them both.

The emphasis in the genre approach lies on differences in types of texts, and not on subject matter, and whole language theorists may feel that aspects of language in social context are neglected. However, genre theory does highlight the need to take into account the various purposes and forms of language, while developing links with subject matter or content, and acknowledging the knowledge of the learner. It alerts us to the need to expose children to factual texts as well as fictional texts. It seems useful to take pertinent aspects of language theory from both approaches in developing our own view of language learning.

HALLIDAY'S SYSTEMIC FUNCTIONAL MODEL OF LANGUAGE

Genre theory largely stems from the work of linguists such as Michael Halliday, who examined language as a system. His systemic functional model of language provides a useful theoretical framework in which to consider language learning, and it also highlights a number of important terms that are frequently used in contemporary educational circles but infrequently defined. Some aspects of Halliday's model have been extended to take on a broader meaning.

Language, according to Halliday, is:
- **functional,** in that it allows us to get things done
- **social,** in that it allows us to communicate with others
- **contextual,** in that the way in which we need to use language and thus the way we use it depends on the sociocultural context.

1 MEANING

Halliday's model describes language in use and highlights the linguistic choices available to language users. It describes how we structure language to make meaning.

2 TEXT

The model emphasises text. Our view of language is very much influenced by our experiences with texts, and Halliday defines text as 'language that is functional. By functional, we mean language that is doing some job in some context.' Text is made of meanings, which are expressed in words or structures, in sounds or written symbols. Text may be seen as product. Text may also be viewed as a process in that a number of choices about how we make meaning are available to us. (Halliday & Hasan 1985, p.10-11)

TRANSACTION

Transaction involves making meaning by giving and receiving knowledge, skills and values through interaction with others. This notion is important, because it recognises that knowledge is not transmitted in a controlled sequence. We need to build on what learners bring to a new situation. Transaction involves a social exchange of meanings where the meanings negotiated actually become some new thing. For instance, when Nita, a Year 3 student, told her peers about the information on houses that she intended to collect, the following interchange of ideas occurred:

Nita: Luke, I'm doing it... interview a person okay. I'm going to ask them where they live, what street they live in... I've got the

suburbs, the streets, the number of the house. Have you got any more?
Luke: Yeah, colour of the house.
Nita: Colour of the house?
James: What kind of car they have?
Nita: That's got nothing to do with the house.
Luke: Colour roof?
Vulcan: What kind of roof?
Nita: Is the house brick or wood?
Luke: You've done well.
Nita: I've got it. Names, where they live, which suburb, what their house is made of, the number of the house. You could do more... fence colour, roof colour...

During the interaction, Nita's ideas for her interviews expanded. She used some of the ideas from her peers but discovered a few of her own. She rejected those that seemed inappropriate. Transaction occurs, a sharing of meanings takes place, and the original idea or meaning is altered and expanded.

TEXT AS DYNAMIC

A text can be defined as meaningful language used for a purpose, whether in spoken or written form. A text is dynamic: it involves transaction and is influenced by the context or situation. The dynamic nature of text is seen in the following interaction between the members of an editing team of Year 2 and 3 children who were preparing to publish a class cookbook for Christmas. As they read over the drafts submitted by their peers they discussed the tense of the verbs in each piece.

Nita: Scrape or scraped.
Mike: Scraped.
Nita: You have to have them all like 'stir' or 'stirred'. Listen, listen... what do you want? 'Stir' or 'stirred' or 'scrape' or 'scraped.' Mike, do you want 'clean' or 'cleaned' or 'scrape' or 'scraped'? Luke?
Luke: Yeah...
Nita: They have to be all the same. Make it this is grated. Do you want 'grate' or 'grated'?
Mike: Grated.
Luke: Yeah, grated.
Nita: That makes sense all right. That can go in the book.

The editing team, spurred on by Nita's insistence, knew that the tense of the writing had to be consistent, so they revised each recipe in line with their decision to use the past tense. Later, however, when they read a few cookbooks in the classroom, they decided to use the present tense. Time to talk about writing, opportunity for flexible decision-making and access to meaningful examples of accessible written texts are all important.

3 GENRE

Genre, or the relationship of the text to the context, constitutes the third aspect of Halliday's model. Part of learning about language entails learning how different texts are organised in order to fulfill their functions. The way in which a text is structured or shaped in order to fulfil its function can be termed **genre**. Genres are goal oriented, enabling people to achieve a given purpose or function. For instance, if one wants to outline how to cook a special dish, it is appropriate to list the ingredients needed and the method or procedure to be followed. The procedural genre is most appropriate in this case. The demands of different contexts determine how language, both written and spoken, is used and for which purposes. This influences the language items selected and, thus, the genre created.

ORAL GENRES

Children generally come to school with control over a range of oral genres. (Green & Green 1991, p.40) For instance, a young child often knows how to retell weekend events, how to describe a favourite food and explain why bedtime should be postponed for an hour or so. Such language learning has occurred incidentally through a range of social contexts, and has also been made explicit by caretakers helping children to use language appropriately according to the demands of the context. (Callaghan & Rothery 1989, p.21)

WRITTEN GENRES

Later, control of language extends to written language. 'When children learn to write, they learn to create genres.' (Christie 1987, p.209)

At the beginning of the school year Vulcan, a Year 2 child, primarily wrote recounts and narratives in his free choice independent writing. When he was exposed to a wider range of genres, he added procedural texts (how to), reports and descriptions to his writing repertoire. He had participated in language use for various purposes and seen the related forms or genres.

LANGUAGE AS CONTEXTUAL

Genres are determined by the sociocultural context: the purposes for which we use language vary according to the goals of the given society. In Nauru there is a strong tradition in storytelling as a form of entertainment. The stories are often recounts based on an actual event. However, the recount is exaggerated to become amusing and a blend of genres occurs. Such stories are highly valued and have evolved over long periods of time. The strong oral tradition of the Nauruan people has meant a limited access to written genres, when compared with our own access and cultural needs, although this is now changing.

GENRE AND IDEOLOGY

Genre is seen to be intimately related to ideology. Heath (1983) demonstrates the cultural differences between several communities which hold various social goals. These goals influence the way in which language is used and the genre that evolves. In Roadville, children are expected to be both information giver and information receiver. Children are expected to retell events and adhere to the truth. (p.165) As a result of the cultural expectations of the community, a recount genre evolves. However, in Trackton the expectations are different. Young children are praised for telling good entertaining stories, giving rise to narrative rather than factual texts. (p.166) The recount genre does not achieve the same importance as it does in Roadville; instead, storytelling and play songs including amusing rhymes and insults are prominent. (pp.175-8) The strong oral tradition of the Trackton people means that there is limited access to written genres.

Harrison and McEvedy (1987) point out that 'Not all cultures are print oriented.' (p.40) They use the example of traditional Aboriginal cultures and state that until recently such cultures had little awareness of print because few Aboriginal languages were written down. According to O'Donoghue (1991), Aboriginal children do well in situations when they can 'exploit their learning style of "learning from watching".' (p.9) He notes that learning by listening can be quite difficult for Aboriginal children. Enemburu (1989) explains how verbal instructions and questions are not common to this learning style. In traditional Aboriginal cultures it is considered impolite to answer questions directly. It follows that a classroom that relies heavily on students learning by listening, and where teachers use instructions and questions to monitor teaching effectiveness, may cause confusion for Aboriginal children.

The impact of differences in cultural ideologies cannot be ignored by teachers.

4 THE RELATIONSHIP BETWEEN TEXT AND CONTEXT

The relationship between text and context is known as **register**. Callaghan and Rothery (1989) say that two contexts exist for any text: the context of the **culture** (genre); and the context of the **situation** which is the relationship between context and text (register). Register involves three variables: field, tenor and mode.

- **field** refers to the subject matter
- **tenor** means the relationship between participants
- **mode** refers to the means of communication (speech or writing)

For example, a writing conference between a teacher and a child about a jointly constructed class text, written in the procedural genre and entitled *Fish, Fish, Fish,* serves to illustrate **register**. The **field** involves the topic of fish, the **tenor** involves the roles of listener and speaker, whilst the **mode** is one of speech. The cultural context is the classroom within the school community and the wider local community. The procedural genre is used as it most appropriate to the purpose of the text given the context.

When language is used, a text is created in response to both the cultural and the situational context. (Christie, Martin & Rothery 1989, p.44) If we are to use language competently, we need to learn to recognise the contexts of the social interaction and make linguistic selections accordingly.

HOW LANGUAGE FUNCTIONS TO MAKE MEANING

Halliday's systemic functional grammar or description attempts to explain the way in which language functions to make meaning. He distinguishes three kinds of meaning:
- experiential (choices for making sense of experiences)
- interpersonal (choices about interaction between language users)
- textual (choices that make links between clauses or sentences, as well as within them, so that a text is constructed)

(Christie, Martin & Rothery 1989, p.46)

Language can be seen as 'a system for making choices for the meanings we wish to convey.' (Callaghan & Rothery 1989, p.36) Halliday's model is functional, in that it takes into account how language is used and how language evolves according to need.

It is significant in that it highlights language:
- in terms of meaning (interpersonal, textual and experiential)
- as not merely for communication, but as also a resource enabling one to function in a given context (Christie 1990)
- as being used in ways dictated by the given sociocultural context
- in terms of how meaning is made when language is used for real purposes. When seen in this light, language cannot be viewed as a set system operating under strict rules
- as dynamic, not static, for as societies change, the social goals and needs of the individuals and communities vary. In order to meet such change, language must grow, adapt and evolve.

Halliday's model also highlights the need for educators to review their own understandings of language learning. It challenges educators who use teaching strategies which do not incorporate genre approaches. For instance, if one of our aims is to help learners become more aware of how language is used for a wide range of purposes within our society, then we need to know this for ourselves. We need to understand how a range of texts function, to be able to identify various genres used, to develop a language to talk about language (or a metalanguage) and to develop explicit teaching strategies enabling both teachers and children to extend their text repertoires.

WHOLE LANGUAGE APPROACHES AND GENRE APPROACHES

We live in an 'essayist' society, (Scollon & Scollon 1981), in that written language, rather than oral language, is emphasised. In order to function effectively in our 'essayist' society, we need to be able to use language for an increasing range of purposes. If we are to prepare learners for such language use, we must provide access to a wide range of text types or genres. Accessible texts which provide a range of information in a variety of text genres are now being produced, and teachers and children have access to a broad spectrum of examples of language used for real purposes.

As teachers demonstrate the purpose of various text types and show how they can be structured, as well as creating texts with students, readers and writers have greater choice when deciding how to make meaning.

AN INTEGRATED CURRICULUM

Different areas of the curriculum create various demands on language use. Educators, therefore, need to provide for language learning across the whole curriculum. An integrated curriculum demonstrates the interdependence of various subject areas. For instance, talking, listening, reading and writing are linked with other curriculum areas, such as social science, science and mathematics, giving rise to the need for a range of texts from all aspects of the curriculum.

Children's natural curiosity and their need for knowledge about the social and physical world must be accommodated. Inquiry-based programs enable us to extend content knowledge as well as develop a broad range of skills associated with data collection, collation and analysis.

A RANGE OF TEXTS

The need for a range of text genres, both oral and written, in our classrooms is now being recognised. Previously there was an overwhelming predominance of fictional texts, and factual written texts were sadly lacking. As Christie points out, 'young children write what they are enabled to write'. (Christie 1987, p.207) The effects of exposure to a limited range of texts was reflected in the writing that emerged from classrooms. Children wrote mainly narrative pieces and recounts, showing the connection between reading and writing.

What we now know about language learning is the result of years of teaching and research by many educators; the cumulative insights of reflective practitioners have led us to our current view. This no doubt will change in time as we build upon what we know in a changing cultural context and its changing demands on our language use.

Access to a range of texts gives children writing choices.

2
GETTING TO KNOW FACTUAL TEXTS

WHY USE FACTUAL TEXTS?

Factual texts constitute a vital part of our classroom programs. Reading, writing and talking about factual texts for real purposes is important for many reasons.

FACTUAL TEXTS ARE REAL

A great deal of factual reading and writing occurs in our everyday lives. At home, for instance, written texts such as shopping lists, timetables, instructions on household appliances, news reports and recipes abound. Factual texts are real in the sense that they have authentic functions and meet actual needs within society — they represent reality and interpretations of reality. As knowledge is tentative and dynamic, we need to update and replace factual texts in terms of what we know at a given time.

FACTUAL TEXTS ARE ENABLING

Our society puts much emphasis on reading and writing. In order to function effectively we need to be able to read and write for a range of purposes, and we need control of a range of oral genres. As teachers, we need to extend children's factual text repertoires so that they are better able to function within society.

It is said that being able to use factual texts effectively is 'empowering'. What does this mean?

The term 'empowerment' is overused and often misused. It is misleading in that it creates images of social power, and whilst being able to read and to write effectively *enables* the individual to function within our society, we do not gain access to the power bases of society just because we can read and write. The term 'enabling' rather than 'empowering' is more useful. Being able to read and write for a range of purposes is enabling in that it makes us better able to function within our society.

FACTUAL TEXTS PROVIDE INFORMATION ABOUT THE WORLD

Factual texts teach us about the physical, social and natural world. Young children have a sense of wonder and a thirst for information about the world which can easily be lost if it is not nurtured. Factual texts can encourage this interest by providing information and stimulating curiosity.

Factual texts allow us to consider the content of our curriculum as well as the processes involved. For instance, by using scientific texts in our reading and writing programs we can explore scientific phenomena as well as examine the related literacy demands. This saves time but, more importantly, makes our reading and writing meaningful, interesting and a part of the quest for knowledge about our world.

FACTUAL TEXTS CAN STIMULATE INQUIRY

Factual texts can be used as a starting point for children's investigations. For instance, a book such as *What Did You Eat Today?* includes information in table form, and this can be used as a guide to tabulating information gained from interviewing people about their eating habits. A Year 2/3 class collated their findings into table form and this became the basis of a class book. Following this, a number of children used interview techniques for data collection and then used the table format from *What Did You Eat Today?* in their own free choice writing. (*This is discussed further in chapter 4, p. 73.*)

Reading and writing such texts with children highlights the nature of inquiry and methods of collecting and presenting information. Children can interview people, record observations and then tabulate, map or graph the results. Learning is occurring by transaction (acquiring knowledge, skills and values through interaction with others).

FACTUAL TEXTS CAN SHOW PURPOSES FOR READING AND WRITING

While we may still have memories of inaccessible texts and boring projects from our own school days, there is now an increasing number of accessible factual texts available, and these can add enjoyment to reading and writing. For instance, Greg, a Year 2 boy, was rather uninterested in reading and writing until he was introduced to books such as *Hidden Animals* and *Animal Clues*. He was particularly drawn to books that used an inquiry format which required him to make a guess. The photographs appealed to him not only because they are beautifully presented but also because he could gain information from them. Greg was very interested in science. He constantly collected and labelled objects from the bush, such as leaves, gumnuts and branches, for the science display. Spurred on by *Bush Secrets*, Greg wrote and took right through to publication his own book: a report about leaves. The commercial text gave him the idea that he could use his knowledge about leaves in his own writing. Factual texts can motivate even a rather uninterested reader and writer by showing that reading and writing can be purposeful.

FACTUAL TEXTS SHOW HOW LANGUAGE WORKS

When students have access to a range of factual texts they can understand how language works for different purposes. With time, they will gain confidence and competence in acquiring information from various text genres. For instance, after much shared reading and explicit talk about tables of contents using *Your Backyard Jungle*, many of Michael Green's Preps knew how to read a table of contents. Later, when Sally selected *An Introduction to Australian Spiders* during DEAR (drop everything and read time) she turned to the table of contents, pointed to the chapter heading 'Where Spiders Live', found the corresponding page number, flipped over to page 7 and began to read. As well as knowing how to find information by using a table of contents, Sally knew that factual reports do not need to be read from cover to cover. She knew that she could begin reading at the page that interested her most and she did just that!

FACTUAL TEXTS EXTEND WRITING OPTIONS

Working with factual texts enables students to see options in their language use. When returning from Horsebend Farm a Year 2/3 class listed their writing options. Luke explained to the class, 'We could write a recount or a report about the animals.' When other possibilities, such as descriptions of specific animals or people, and procedural texts like 'How to find your way around the farm', were listed on a chart by the teacher the children realised there were possibilities far beyond the usual recount.

Their growing awareness of an increased number of writing options was also apparent in the terms that they used to describe writing. For

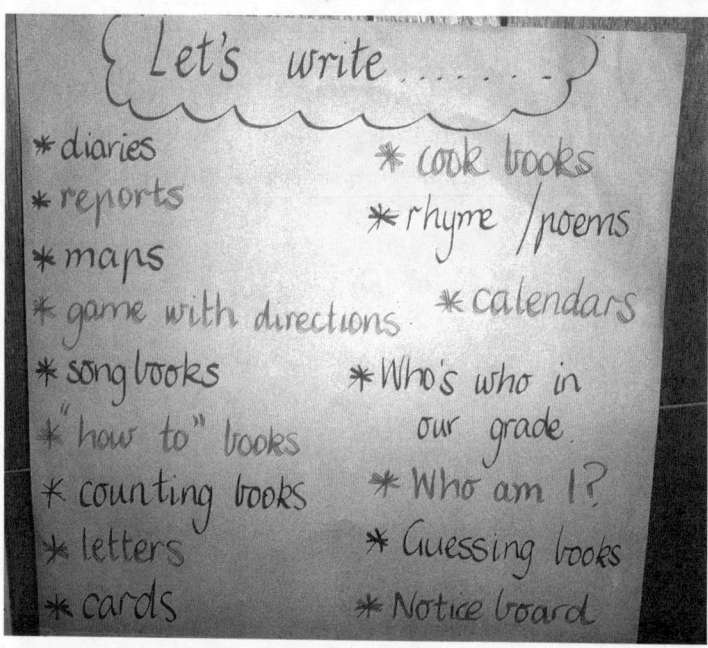

A class list demonstrates possible writing options.

instance, Luke constantly corrected others about using the term 'story writing' (a relic from the year before) to describe writing. This occurred later in the year, after much teacher emphasis on the term 'writing' rather than 'story writing' to talk about writing. Vulcan asked, 'When are we having story writing?' Luke demonstrated his awareness of the functions of writing when he said, 'We don't just write stories.' Luke's changing understanding of terms revealed the effect of teacher talk and explicit teaching on both his writing growth and his oral language.

FACTUAL TEXTS PROMOTE PURPOSEFUL TALK

When making decisions about the most appropriate genre to use, children need to consider their purpose for writing and the intended audience. Teachers can alert children to the need to think about these aspects and demonstrate how to consider them during whole class discussions, such as introductory sessions and sharetime, and during conferences between teacher and a child, or teacher and small group, or peers. In time, children will ask each other questions, often using many of those used by the teacher. Such purposeful talk can be promoted by asking questions, such as:

What are you writing?
What is your purpose?
What kind of information are you trying to provide?
What style of writing would be best for this? Why?
Whom are you writing for?

Who will read this piece of writing?
What will they be looking for?
What will hold their interest?
What will make the information accessible or easy to read?
Are there any books that you can use to help you with ideas for your writing?
Are there any books that you can use to work out how to make the information easy for the reader to find?

This kind of talk greatly expands children's use of terminology related to the writing process. At the start of the school year in a Year 2/3, Vulcan announced that he wanted to be a publisher but, when asked to explain, it was discovered that he meant an author. He was exploring the terms that occurred as a natural part of our reading and writing. However, later in the year he stated that he wanted to be an editor and 'check writing before it's published.' When Vulcan reflected on his writing over the year and what he had learnt, he said: 'I know how to do true books. I like publishing books. I know how to do a glossary.'

Many children, like Vulcan, revealed an understanding of the various roles within writing, such as editor, author, publisher and illustrator. Their talk also indicated an awareness of the features of various written texts, such as glossaries, tables of contents, indexes and copyright signs.

By using these terms, the children discovered how to apply them appropriately. If a term was misused, someone was usually there to provide the correct form or term. When Vulcan was confused about the meaning of the term non-fiction, Luke provided an appropriate explanation and offered the less confusing term, factual books. The children had become more explicit in their talk and were better able to help each other by asking more demanding questions and finding detailed solutions. A language to talk about language was developing.

FACTUAL TEXTS INCREASE TEXT REPERTOIRES

Writing and reading, as well as talking about factual texts, increases students' repertoires as they become aware of language use in a range of contexts. In time, students begin to 'read as writers' searching for ideas for their own writing as they read. As Mick, a Year 3 child said, 'I look in the books. . . some books give me ideas. I think I can do something like that for my book.'

Titles are known as examples of various genres. For instance, *Kids in the Kitchen* is easily recognised as a 'how to' or a procedural text, while *An Introduction to Australian Spiders* is identified as a report. Students can consult these when they need examples on which to base their own writing. When writing, they begin to 'write as readers', keeping the audience in mind by carefully considering the inclusion of appropriate locational devices, like the table of contents, to make their information accessible.

Ideas about factual texts are readily shared as children become more confident and competent in using them. For instance, Luke learnt how to write a glossary for his report about the Melbourne Cup which included new terminology. He then recommended that his friend Mick, who was writing a report about motorbikes, include a glossary in his writing.

WHAT ARE FACTUAL TEXTS?

The tentative, dynamic nature of knowledge means that factual texts represent interpretations of the world as we know it at a given time. For instance, before 1969 many factual texts reported human exploits in outer space. When Neil Armstrong first stepped onto the surface of the moon in July 1969, existing information about space exploits needed to be extended to include this event. Given that knowledge changes over time, there is a continual need to update and replace factual texts as new knowledge and fresh insights are gained.

The term factual texts, rather than that of 'non-fiction', seems more appropriate as it refers to what such texts are rather than what they are not.

It is useful to have a guideline or set of workable definitions for a range of text genres. Martin (1985) suggests six main types of factual writing, and this has since been extended by adding two other factual genres. The main types of factual texts are recount, procedure, description, report, discussion, argument, explanation and exposition. These can be found in both oral and written forms. The purpose of the text determines its genre. Figure 2.2 offers a starting point for getting to know factual texts. It can be used as a checklist to monitor the range of genres that has been used.

Note how the term exposition is used. On occasion it has been used to mean factual texts, but this is inappropriate. Exposition is a type of factual text, not a term that directly equates to factual texts. Exposition involves a sophisticated use of language for purposes that are usually socially or scientifically significant. This text genre often involves higher order thinking in relation to levels of knowledge.

theory	exposition
generalisation	argument, discussion
conclusion	explanation, report
concept	recount, description, procedure
fact	basis of all factual genres

Figure 2.1 A hierarchy of knowledge related to factual genres

GETTING TO KNOW FACTUAL TEXTS

Genre	Purpose	Oral form	Written form
RECOUNT	Retells past events	'Morning talk' or 9 o'clock chatter	Diary writing *On the weekend ...* Excursion recap *Last week we visited ...* Historical journey *In 1788 ...*
PROCEDURE	Supplies details of how something is done	Directions to school office to a visitor	Recipe *How to make pizza.* Game instructions *How to play chess.*
DESCRIPTION	Tells what something specific is like	News time *My new kitten is black.* Oral language game *Describe a mystery object in a bag.*	Classified ads *Car for sale* Who am I? *Guessing the person, object or thing from a description*
REPORT	Tells what a group of things is like	Class talk *The bears at the zoo were ...* TV documentary	Factual books *A book of animal reports* Pamphlets *All about heart attacks*
ARGUMENT	Provides reasons why a judgement is made One side of the argument is given	Persuasive talk *I want to use the computer because ...*	Letter to the editor *Why our school needs a crossing*

Figure 2.2 An overview of factual genres (continues on next page)

Genre	Purpose	Oral form	Written form
EXPLANATION	How something works or the reason(s) why something is the way it is	Explaining how the borrowing system works Why an object floats or sinks	Trade manuals Car manuals Why people engage in war
DISCUSSION	Provides both sides of an argument	Class discussion Debates	Newspaper article *The pros and cons of drinking coffee*
EXPOSITION	Takes a stance on a socially and/or scientifically significant issue	Group presentation *Why we must save the whales*	Government paper *Unemployed Youth* Environmental interest group paper *The greenhouse effect*

Figure 2.2 (cont.)

This hierarchy of knowledge shows facts as the basis of all factual genres.

- For instance, the following statement is a **fact**:
  The first man landed on the moon in 1969.

- It could provide the basis of a **description**, with additional information, when the conditions on the moon are described:
  The moon surface was pitted with circular craters.

- The basis of a personal **recount** is provided for those of us old enough to remember:
  I remember the excitement when we were sent home from school to watch the event on TV.

- A **procedural** text could be written, for instance:
  A log book detailing how the space journey occurred hour by hour.

- At the next level of knowledge a **conclusion** could be drawn:
  The landing on the moon was such a significant news event that our local paper reported the event in great detail and for a few days other news seemed insignificant by comparison.

- An **explanation** could follow:
  How the mass media gained the photographs and information for the public.

- The basis for a **report** is also provided when considering *space travel in general*.

- A **generalisation** could be formed, such as:
  The most significant event in the history of space travel occurred in 1969 when Neil Armstrong became the first person to land on the moon.
  This generalisation forms the basis of an **argument** as others might argue the significance of other exploits in space.

- A **discussion** of *the pros and cons of space travel* could then emerge.

- A **theory** of the likelihood of finding other lifeforms in space may follow. This could form the basis of an **exposition**: *the impact of space exploits on other possible life forms.* As an exposition is a sophisticated genre, it occurs infrequently in primary school.

While children need to be exposed to whole range of factual genres, the way in which this occurs will vary according to the level of complexity of the genre and the children's experience with oral and written genres.

Martin classifies according to whether the text refers to the **specific** or the **general**. This is particularly useful for getting to know factual texts and learning how to alert children to different between different genres. It has been extended to include explanations and discussions.

Focus	Specific	General
EVENT	recount	procedure
THING	description explanation	report
LINE OF THOUGHT	argument discussion	exposition

Figure 2.3 Classifying according to specific or general reference

Note that the term *thing* in this classification may refer to people, animals, plants and/or objects:

RECOUNT

As Christie (1987) pointed out, recounts and narratives are the most commonly used genres in the writing of children in primary schools. This is particularly evident in the early years of school.

The following diary entry written by Luke (Year 3), a keen football fan, provides a recount of weekend events.

This genre is often found in diaries or journals.

A MATTER OF FACT

On Saturday I went to the Football to see FITZROY and footscray Fitzroy lost by I point it was a good game up to Quarter time Footscray were in front by I point the Quarter started Fitzroy kicked 3 goals I was so happy I was jumping up and down there were five minutes to go I thort we had it won there something awful happened Footscray went wild there was only I miniut togo and the sirin went

What an exciting diary entry. You are a great sports reporter.

PROCEDURE

Our jointly constructed class book entitled *Fish, Fish, Fish* was an example of a procedural text. Chapter 4 outlined the procedure to follow when cleaning a fish tank:

CHAPTER 4.   CLEANING THE FISH TANK.

```
When you clean the fish tank you should never use detergent
You can clean the fish tank with a magnet.
You put half of the magnet on the inside and the other half
on the outside of the tank.
When you get the fish and the water is dirty, you should
always put clean water in or the fish will die.
Clean everything before you get new fish.
You can also clean the fish tank with a clean cloth or a
t-towel as long as it doesn't have detergent on it.
Clean the rocks until they are bright and shiny.
```

DESCRIPTION

The following description written by Vulcan (Year 2) in his book entitled *Mystery Food* entices the reader to make a guess about the object being described:

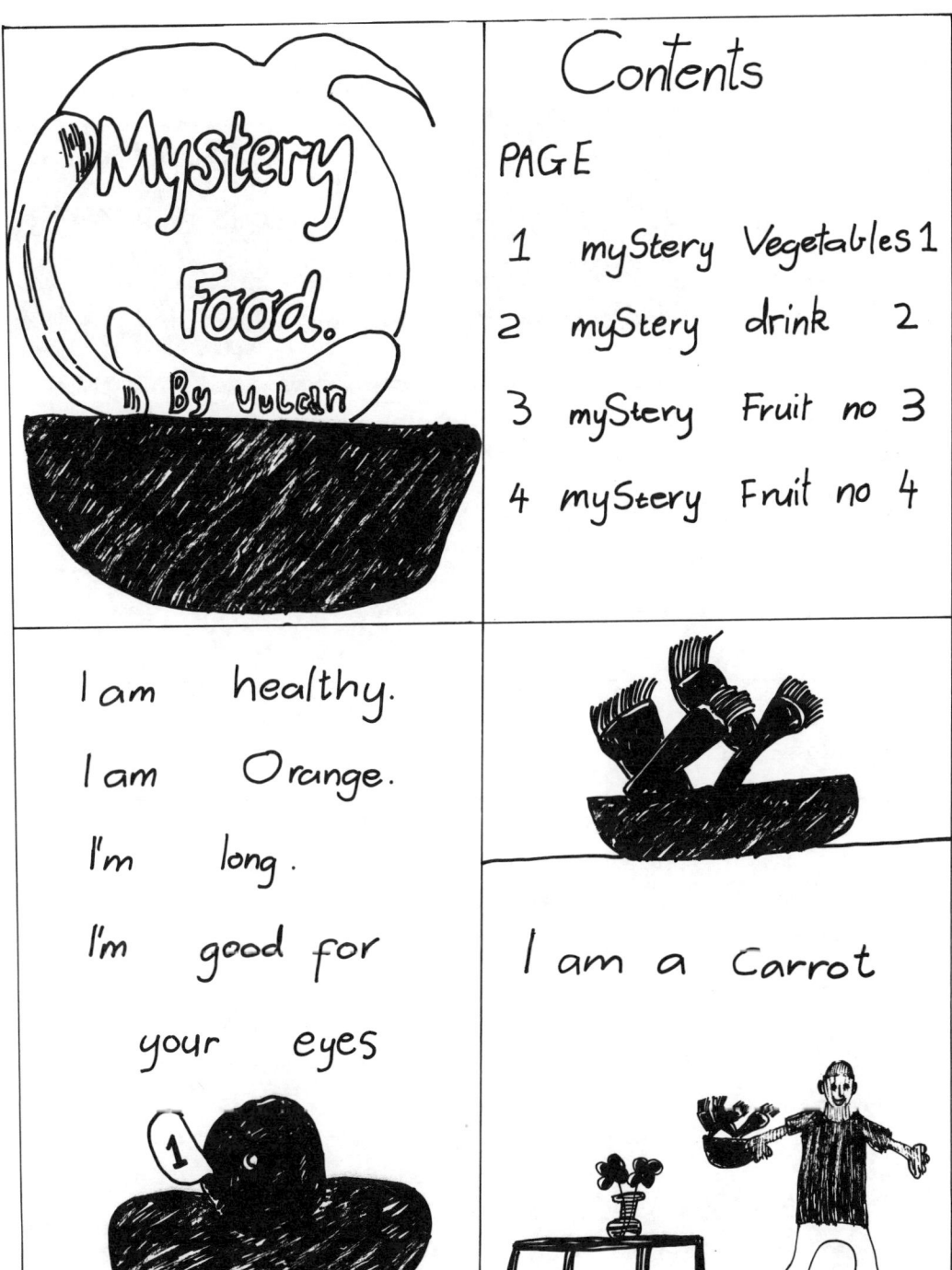

REPORT
Nita (Year 3) wrote this report about cats:

A report about CATS
Reporter: Nita   Date: 14.9.'89
Cats have whiskers so they will know if they will fite into small places. Their whiskers are the biggest part of their body. Their is part of there. The tail helps them to jump and balance. They have two eyes that are very important. They have one on one side and another on the other side so they can see in every direction. Cats purr when they they are happy. A car picks up sounds that are very far away and they know what direction it's coming from. This Animal has claws to tear meat apart, kill mice and dig.

ARGUMENT
Ross (Year 6) wrote an argument about school uniforms:

School Uniforms

School uniforms should not be compulsary for a A number of reasons.

First of all,
  When your uniform is in the washing machine, it might not be able to dry on time.

Secondly,
  Most uniforms are dull and not colourful.

Thirdly,
  Everybody in the school would look the same so you might not be able to tell each other apart.

Fourthly, Some uniforms don't suit some people.

Fifthly, Some families might not be able to afford school uniforms especially if there are a number of school children in the family.

These are five reasons why school uniforms should not be compulsary in schools.

EXPLANATION
Jane and Samantha (Year 6) wrote this explanation of why people read Baby Sitters books:

Baby-Sitters Books,
People read baby-sitters books to find out what it's like to baby sit. They also read them because it tells you things about real life. The ~~baby~~ baby-sitters books are also interesting to read because of the charaters personalty for instences: Claudia likes ant, junk food etc She also has a grandmother who understands her and listens to her problems and is there when claudia needs her. When you read the Baby-sitters books it's sort of like your ~~the per charcles~~ main charater in all the books. You can alsa I can things like the way ~~they~~ solve their promblem the way ~~there~~ they do things and also from words you ~~sound~~ hardly ever use in your for instence vacation, assumed, compliment, appreciation etc... The ~~baby~~ -sitters books descrcb the charaters that come and go throughout the book. These are the resions why people read them!

A MATTER OF FACT

DISCUSSION
Gina (Year 6) wrote this discussion about the legislation of guns:

GUNS.

GUNS SHOULD NOT BE LEGALIZED!

Some people believe that guns should be legalized and easy to get. Some people like to have guns to protect their property. For Instance, If there are foxes that bother them or kill their animals they might need a gun so they could shoot them It is very dangerous to walk alone at night so that is why some people believe that they need a gun.

However many people believe that guns should not be legalized. If a baby or a small child found a gun He or she wouldn't know what a gun was or even what it was used for. So he or she might accidently pull the trigger and do harm to something or somebody. If guns were legal and easy to get people might just go ahead and use them for no logical reason. They might commit a few murders or even commit suicide. If a gun fell Into the hands of the wrong people it could be DEADLY and DANGEROOS. Think again about guns. they should __NOT__ be legalized!!!!!!!!

TEXTUAL OVERLAP

The overview must be seen as a guideline only. The discrete, rigid boundaries shown in figure 2.2 do not always exist. It is possible to find other text genres that do not fit neatly into this classification, and at times, a blending of text genres occurs. This may happen when:

- the purpose is unclear
- the language user is exploring and gaining competence in a particular genre
- the boundaries between genres overlap
  For instance, an explanation refers to how something works, whereas procedural texts refer to how something is done. At times there is a fine line between the two. When explaining how the library borrowing system works, the procedure of borrowing is likely to be made explicit.
- there is more than one purpose (multiple purposes)
  It is not uncommon for recount to be blended with narrative. This occurs when the writer has two purposes: to retell an event and to entertain the reader. As a result, the truth may be exaggerated so that the event is seen as more interesting. When Luke wrote the following article for a class newspaper, the piece was based on an actual event but was exaggerated to add impact and to promote his expertise in golf.

THE YOUNG STAR GOLFER by Sports Reporter Luke Watson

In Australia, there is a young star Golfer. His name is LUKE WATSON The young star played 18 holes at Craigeburn. He had a 127 because he had been practising every week. How amazing! Could he be as good as Greg Norman?

"I wish," said LUKE.

SELECTING FACTUAL TEXTS

It is important that we select **considerate** written texts. Kantor, Anderson and Armbruster (1983) first used the term 'considerate' in reference to textbooks. The term is useful in that it makes us examine the qualities that make a book accessible to the reader.

WHAT IS A CONSIDERATE FACTUAL TEXT?

According to Morris (1989), considerate texts help to facilitate learning as they have a well-organised structure, well-developed concepts, follow logically, keep the intended audience in mind and use appropriate language. This provides a solid basis for developing selection criteria.

A SELECTION CHECKLIST

Figure 2.4 highlights important criteria to consider when selecting considerate factual texts. It uses Morris's headings and incorporates some criteria summarised by Huck (1989). The list is not exhaustive and each element may not apply to every factual text.

CONCEPTUAL DEVELOPMENT

Factual texts must provide up-to-date information supported by facts known at the time. However, a considerate factual text supplies more than a list of facts. It will develop the information into conclusions, generalisations and/or theories, encouraging the reader to think independently about the information rather than to merely learn a number of facts by rote. The interrelationships between the concepts should be made clear via relevant, current and interesting information.

SEQUENCE

The content must be logically sequenced so that if the reader reads the complete text from cover to cover they can follow the accumulation and increasing complexity of the information. This is particularly important in procedural texts. If the sequence is incorrect or unclear the information will be misinterpreted. In some circumstances, such as in scientific experiments, the consequences could be dangerous. Some factual texts, such as reports about plant growth and recounts of historical events, rely heavily on time sequences. If these are not organised carefully the information gained is likely to be inaccurate.

AUDIENCE

The purpose of the writing must be clear. For instance, the aim of a piece of writing may be to tell how to bake a cake. Having determined this purpose, the writer can then consider the audience. Will they be experienced cooks? If not, minimal prior knowledge must be assumed. Cooking terms and measurement abbreviations must be made explicit. If the intended audience is to be children, the writer would then need to reflect on the kind of cakes that children would be interested in cooking. Safety precautions or kitchen rules would need to be included. As well as relevance and appropriateness, appeal to the audience must be considered. Texts need to include interesting content and to be attractively designed to motivate the reader.

STRUCTURE

The structure of a text is vital. Considerate texts are clearly and logically laid out with complete 'chunks' of text, appropriate headings, and helpful locational devices such as tables of contents. If these components are lacking, the text is not considerate; the reader must try to impose such text markers in order to make sense of the text.

STRUCTURE:	• clear and consistent layout • complete 'chunks' of text • appropriate and clearly arranged headings and sub-headings • easily accessible locational devices, such as table of contents, index
CONCEPTS:	• well developed into generalisations supported by facts so that the information makes sense and is true • explain interrelationships between concepts • provide relevant, current and interesting information
SEQUENCE:	• logically ordered
AUDIENCE:	• purpose kept in mind • cater for the needs and interests of the intended audience • attractive, inviting layout
LANGUAGE:	• title, headings and information in language appropriate to the genre and subject area • not simplistic, but vivid and interesting • glossary for subject area jargon • supported by 'illustrations' appropriate to a factual text, which may include clear captions • 'illustrations' located in proximity to the relevant section of the text • use of non-sexist, non-racist language

Figure 2.4 A checklist for the selection of factual texts (Green and Green 1991, pp. 40-1)

LANGUAGE

The language used in a factual text must be appropriate to its purpose. For instance, when writing a formal report it could be inappropriate to use the personal pronoun 'I', whereas this could be suitable in a recount.

The language should not be watered down or made overly simplistic. Appropriate terminology about a given curriculum area can be learned through factual texts. For instance, when working with spiders, Michael's Preps read about, and then used in their own classroom interaction, terms like abdomen (rather than stomach) and spinnerets. A glossary helps to make new or specific terminology accessible. If illustrations are included, they need to be appropriate in terms of form. Photographs provide glimpses of the real world, and clear captions help to make them accessible and make links with the text. Reading is made easier when illustrations are located close to the relevant information. Cookbooks that provide photographs for recipes located in other parts of the book can be frustrating especially for young readers.

The use of non-sexist, non-racist language is essential.

PUTTING THE CRITERIA TO THE TEST: A CONSIDERATE TEXT

Mice, Mice, Mice is an example of a considerate text which was used with a Year 2/3 class. (Strategies are described in chapter 4.) The book is well organised, providing a clearly set out table of contents which reveals a logically sequenced list of relevant chapter headings. A system of headings, and a clear, consistent layout makes information easier to find. Information is not fragmented but provided in whole 'chunks.' For instance, information about one aspect of keeping mice is kept to a double page. This layout helps the reader absorb the information because it provides a 'whole picture.'

The purpose of the text is to provide the reader with information about keeping mice. The intention is made clear from the start by the title and is supported by the chapter headings. The text is procedural: outlining how to care for mice. Appropriate concepts, such as needs and

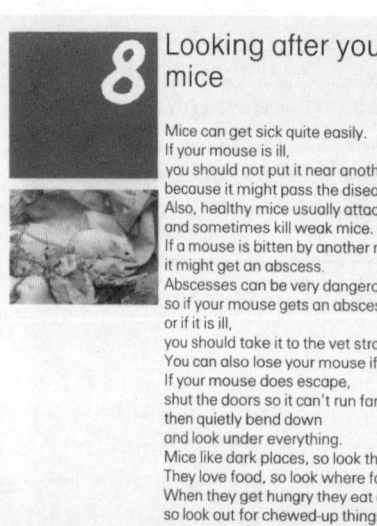

8 Looking after your mice

Mice can get sick quite easily.
If your mouse is ill,
you should not put it near another mouse
because it might pass the disease on.
Also, healthy mice usually attack
and sometimes kill weak mice.
If a mouse is bitten by another mouse,
it might get an abscess.
Abscesses can be very dangerous,
so if your mouse gets an abscess
or if it is ill,
you should take it to the vet straight away.
You can also lose your mouse if it escapes.
If your mouse does escape,
shut the doors so it can't run far,
then quietly bend down
and look under everything.
Mice like dark places, so look there.
They love food, so look where food is.
When they get hungry they eat anything,
so look out for chewed-up things
and you might find your mouse.
If you take care of your mouse
it could live up to 3 years.

Keep it out of a draught so it won't get sick
and keep it warm and dry.
You should look after your mouse
because it is a proper pet.

environment, are well developed and the information follows logically. The information makes sense because it is written clearly and is up-to-date. The reader has the opportunity to learn something new and the intended audience is kept in mind.

Mice, Mice, Mice was written by primary school children for other primary school children. The language is appropriate. The text is supported by photographs which match the text on the given page and provide appropriate illustrations. Clues about the process of writing the book are given in the blurb which outlines the use of cross-age partners as editors. The text is more than merely considerate; it invites readers to write their own texts by revealing how this text was constructed.

Index

baby mice 5, 19, 20
bedding 7
biting 14, 22
breeding 5
cage 5, 6, 7, 10, 12, 17, 20
cleaning 6, 9, 10, 12, 20
climbing 13, 15, 17
drinking 7, 13
droppings 17
eating 8, 9
escaping 5, 9, 22
feeding 7, 8, 20
floor 6, 7, 12
food 7, 8, 9, 14, 15, 22
health 5
holding 10, 14, 18

milk 20
nest(ing) 19, 20
picking up 10, 14, 15
playing 7, 10, 16, 18
scratching 14
sickness 8, 22
sleeping 7
smelling 9, 15
suckling 20
tail 10, 14, 21
taming 14, 16
teeth 8
toys 7
treats 8
water 7, 8, 12

3
STARTING OFF WITH FACTUAL TEXTS

A Glimpse from a Prep Classroom

◆

EXPECTATIONS
For the children in Michael Green's Prep classroom exposure to factual texts occurs from the beginning of the school year. Just as Michael expects that each child will be a listener, talker, reader and writer from the outset, he expects that each child will be interested in listening to, talking about, reading and writing factual texts. To him factual texts are an important part of a balanced program, and the need to build upon oral genres and move into written genres exists from the beginning of the year.

Michael expects that each child will:
- expect to and want to learn to read and write
- talk freely about their learning
- feel free to make mistakes and to take learning 'risks'
- discover new challenges in their learning
- realise that language is used for many purposes
- gain increasing control of a range of genres, both oral and written
- work co-operatively, taking a range of roles
- value the contributions of others
- take increasing responsibility for their own learning

FROM THE BEGINNING OF SCHOOL
Children begin school with a variety of experiences of spoken and written language. A significant number of children in Michael's class

STARTING OFF WITH FACTUAL TEXTS

come with little English. All arrive at school with some degree of control of a range of oral genres (in English or their home language). Most bring some awareness of written language, gained primarily from reading experiences with stories and rhymes, and from exposure to environmental print, particularly through advertising, such as McDonald's logos. Some have experimented with writing, by 'scribbling', and writing their first names.

Most children expect to learn to read and write from the first day at school. Michael believes that it is essential that this expectation is met as much as possible. From day one, opportunities to read and write (and of course, talk) occur daily. The children are encouraged to read and to write in whatever form they can. Early attempts are celebrated: when a group of children wrote about how they made a cake, they read it to the whole class. The writing took pride of place in the centre of the room for all to see. The variation in writing development is apparent but all is seen as significant.

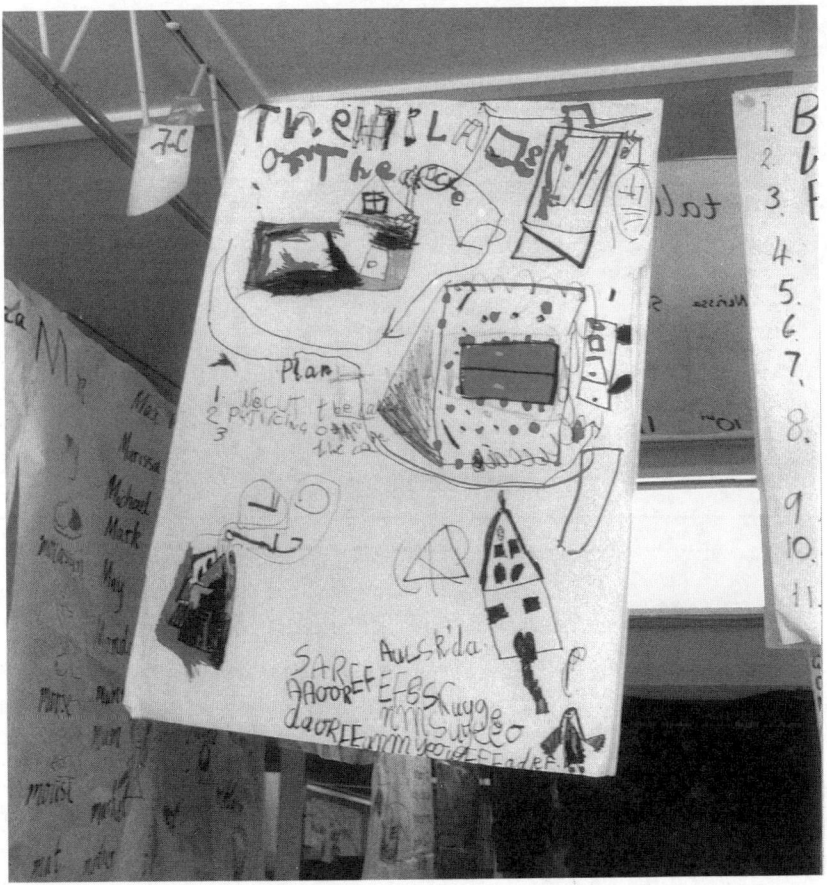

The children's work is displayed for all to see.

A MATTER OF FACT

PHYSICAL ASPECTS: 'WATCH YOUR HEAD'

Michael's classroom is full of children's work. The children view their room as special and it is. Posters hang from the ceiling, a huge earthworm lines a wall, a play corner houses many treasures, the chalkboard is largely hidden by posters and children's writing, construction materials spill over in one corner, a little shape house invites a game or a quiet moment while Jack and the Beanstalk moves up and down to welcome those who enter the room.

An environment is created where the children feel they belong.

The room is inviting. Michael and the children have created a happy, working, comfortable and interesting environment. Books of all kinds (stories, rhymes, factual texts, dictionaries. . .) fill the shelves, the blackboard ledge and the reading nook, and are easily reached by the children. The room is brimming with work produced by the children themselves. Michael believes strongly that the room must be a place where the children feel they belong. 'The room must be for the children. I don't want a room decorated with 25 perfect butterflies that I have cut out. That proves nothing except that I perhaps don't value the work of the children. I do value their work and I believe that a way to show them this is to display as much of their work as I can. As well as showing that their work is important, the displays provide reference points or reminders of things we have done.'

The displays might not be 'perfect'. The gigantic earthworm made of paper may look somewhat 'mysterious' and in need of explanation to an outsider. Michael allows the children to display their work proudly and to participate in selecting display items. For many children displaying a piece of writing on the wall, after sharing with the class, is as far as they proceed with publication. For others, publication is taken further into chart and/or book making. The extent of the process depends on the needs of the child at the time.

Perfection is not the criterion for displaying items.

THE PHYSICAL SET-UP

Michael plans the layout of the room deliberately. He sees the layout of the room as vitally important to the way in which the room operates and to the environment that is created. The physical layout must allow for:
- work with materials on the floor
- group work and flexibility in groupings
- child choice regarding working area
- easy movement around the room
- access to resources for children and teacher
- a relaxed, comfortable environment

- room for children from other classes (such as during cross-age tutoring)

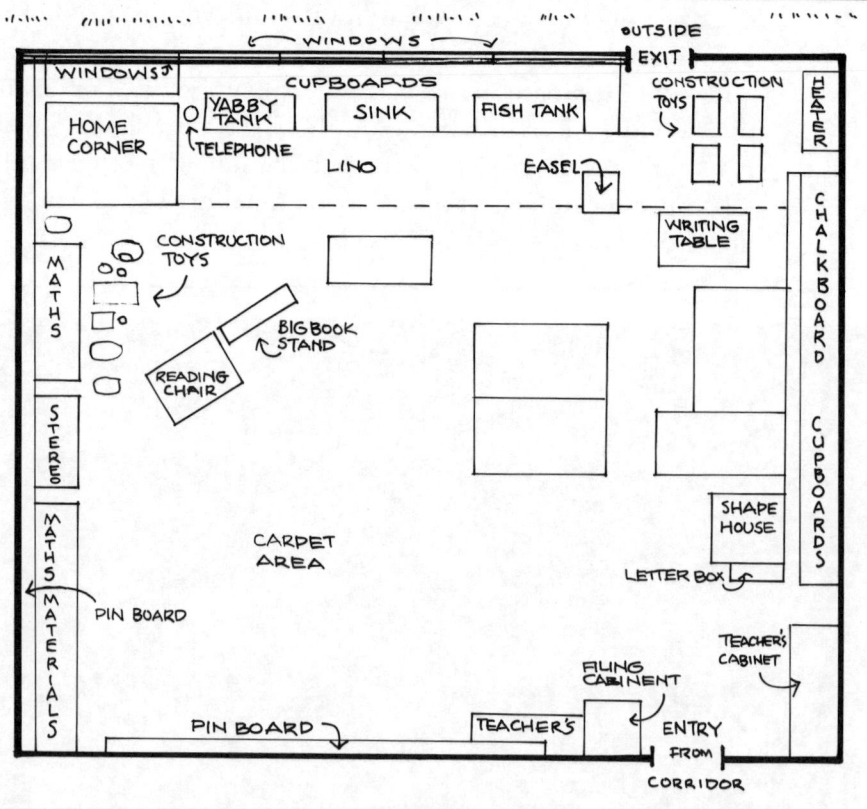

Figure 3.1 The physical layout of Michael's Prep classroom

AN EMPHASIS ON TALKING AND LISTENING

Michael ensures that he is constantly demonstrating how language works in authentic contexts. Much of this is done through classroom talk centred around writing and reading both fictional and factual texts. According to Michael, the opportunity for talking and listening between teacher and child, as well as between children, is particularly crucial for early language experiences. This need, however, never ceases to be a consideration for teachers working with children of all ages. Opportunity for talking and listening, as well as constant feedback, encourages and enables children to begin to use texts independently.

GETTING INTO WRITING: WRITING AND TALKING

Some children arrive at school reluctant to write. This problem is usually short lived as the children realise the positive feedback that early efforts receive. Michael encourages children to 'get into writing' by using the following strategies:

TEACHER AS SCRIBE

At times Michael scribes for children who want to see the correct form under their own writing.

> W Y O Y O W S T S E A H N O C C
> We put some dirt in first.
> We put the seeds in.
> Then we water it.

Michael is reluctant to act as a scribe unless the child has made an attempt at writing. 'Otherwise,' Michael explains, 'the children rely on me to write and this becomes an expectation. If this becomes a habit it can be difficult to break. I want to encourage the children to write independently and to feel that they control their writing.'

A WRITING TABLE

Another handy way to help children get into writing is to establish a writing table. At the start of the year it is very hectic when all children are writing and when many are needing reassurance from a teacher. The writing table eases this problem and also provides a fun way to write. Over a week each child is expected to write at the writing table at least once.

Michael explains how this works:

> *Usually about four children come to the table at once. Each begins to write and I move around talking to each child in turn. I ask each child to read what they have written and then I respond in writing. While I am writing I verbalise what I am doing. For instance, I might say 'I need a capital for the start of a sentence. . . Oh, I must remember to leave a space between the words.' What is really happening is that I am providing a running commentary to make my thoughts explicit as I write. On paper, a written dialogue occurs between each child and me. The children love this and it is useful as I can make clear what happens when writing. I often make deliberate errors and cross them out so that they know that it is okay to make a mistake.'*

The following written conversation between Michael and Naomi occurred late in the year:

Dear Mr. Green,
have you got farres? NO NOT AT THE MOMENT, BUT I HOPE I HAVE A PUPPY SOON, MAYBE NEXT YEAR Have you a dog at home? NO BUT I HAVE SOME FISH a fish theis are sad bid My brother killed tow. HOW DID HE KILL THE FISH? yes! HOW? Same has befor? HE LIFTED THEM OUT! yes he did? WHAT DID YOUR DAD SAY? he yelled furieslly.

DIARY WRITING

Diary writing is a regular part of the school program from the first week of the year. Children are encouraged to write freely in their diaries at least once a week. Michael asks the children to read their writing and he responds on paper to each individual, talking as he writes to make his response clear. Initially most children write recounts about their weekend experiences or events at school.

Later in the year some begin to write in other genres. For instance, after an excursion to the zoo, Steven wrote a description of a giraffe using an animal from the class zoo set.

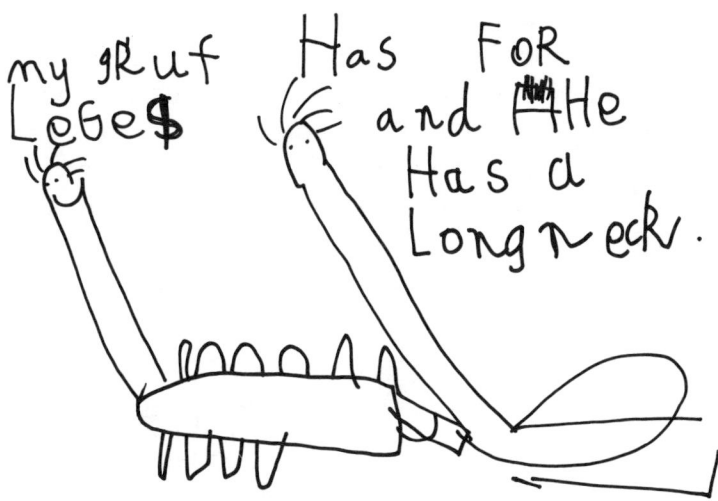

Each entry is dated so that by the end of the year a record of each child's writing growth is readily available.

LETTER WRITING

Letter writing is a particularly useful way to engage children in purposeful writing. A letterbox is established in the room early in the year and correspondence with others, such as cross-age partners, parents and staff, occurs regularly. Letter writing is often demonstrated to the whole group in the form of a wall letter. Michael finds that he needs to work with each child individually to demonstrate how a personal letter is presented.

Letter writing is a great way to begin factual writing as most children see others around them writing letters for various purposes. Paul, who had seen his mother write absence notes to the teacher, decided to write his own on returning to school.

Although a standard letter format has not been used, the intention is clear and a message is conveyed.

Opportunities for purposeful writing and demonstrating appropriate letter formats are constantly taken. For instance, when the class was involved in a wheel-a-thon to raise money for the school, the idea of writing to parents was discussed. Naomi volunteered for the task and wrote this letter, which was then duplicated and distributed to thank parents for their donations.

Dear Thank you For your Donation For Mr. greens bike ride. The money will halp our School. love from Prep.G

GETTING INTO READING: READING AND TALKING

Studies of early 'book talk' that occurs at home have emphasised the importance of such talk in children's language learning. For instance, Ninio and Bruner (1978) studied the early forms of 'dialogue' occurring between mother and child in 'book reading' (or shared reading). They highlighted the ways in which mothers helped the child to participate. Such dialogue was seen as providing scaffolding structures to support the child's learning.

Michael aims to provide similar scaffolds to support the children in their language learning. Of course, the intimacy and closeness of the home shared-book reading cannot be replicated. However, there are opportunities to invite children to participate in shared-book reading of both fictional and factual texts. This occurs in various ways: on a one-to-one basis, in small groups and with the whole class.

STARTING OFF WITH FACTUAL TEXTS

Shared-book reading provides scaffold to support children in their language learning.

Particularly in the early weeks of a new Prep year, there is much shared and individual reading of fictional texts, especially those using repetition and rhyme. A shared-book reading session of the fictional big book *Who Will Be My Mother?* gave rise to the following interaction. The children were seated together on the floor in a tight huddle while Michael sat on a small chair. All children were close to the book. The text was familiar to the children but Michael, on this occasion, chose to mask a number of words to encourage prediction. (Italic text indicates reading from the book.)

All: *Who will be my mother? Mother sheep died. Lamb had no mother. 'Mama, mama,' cried lamb. 'Who will be my mother? Lamb went to the —*
Child & others: Horse.
T: Are you sure?
Chn: Yes.
T: How do you know?
Child: Because that's a horse.
T: It is a horse. And what's this up here?
Chn: A horse.
T: It's a special horse. It's a baby horse. What do you call it?
Child: Donkey.
T: No... ha, ha.. a donkey. No.
Child: I know.

43

T: No.
Child: I know.
T: What's a baby horse called?
Child: Stallion.
Child: Calf.
Child: A calf.
Child: Stable.
Child: Stable.
T: No. A calf...
T: I'm not going to show you that yet.
Child: Aaah, ha.
T: A calf is a baby cow. A foal is a baby horse.
Chn: Wooooah.
T: So you think it is a horse under there?
Chn: Yeah.
T: What would it start with if it was horse?
Chn: H.
T: Let's have a look.
Chn: It is. Yes!
[Break in transcript]
T: Let's just try. *Lamb went to the —*
Child: Bull.
Chn: Rabbit.
T: It fits. It fits. Let's have a look and see if we're right.
Chn: Yes!
T: Lamb. Yes, you're right.
All: *Lamb went to the rabbit.*
Chn: Rabbit! Rabbit! Rabbit!
T: Well, over here he said *'Bull, bull. . .'* And over here he said *'Horse, horse. . .'* Over the page he should say . . .
Child: Somebody didn't take care of it.
Child: Rabbit.
T: He should say
All: *'Rabbit, rabbit.'*
T: Let's have a look.
Child: Rabbit.
Chn: Yes!
All: *'Rabbit, rabbit, will you be my mother?' 'I am a rabbit,' said the rabbit. 'I can't be your mother.'*
Child: Yes he would.
All: *Lamb went to the hen. 'Hen, hen, will you be my mother?' 'I am a hen,' said the hen. 'I can't be your mother.'*
Child: Because he's got to look after 12 chickens.
T: Got to look after 12 chickens, can't be a lamb's mother either.
(Green, Leovold, McGregor, and McNamara 1991, pp.24-6)

STARTING OFF WITH FACTUAL TEXTS

The reading was very lively and occurred very quickly. This shared-book experience, which lasted for about four to five minutes, was the introductory phase of a morning session and was followed by a number of activities related to the text.

THE PATTERN OF THE CLASSROOM DISCOURSE

A pattern of interaction or classroom discourse is clearly established by Michael's use of directives, such as 'Let's have a look.' This is accompanied by questions such as, 'How do you know?' Such explicit talk invites the children to look closely at the text to test the predictions that they are making as they read, as well as thinking about the way in which they gain information. The talk provides implicit information about the reading process in terms of how to read (procedural) and what reading is (substantive).

Later Michael directs the children to look at the picture cues in the text and questions such as 'What would it start with if it was horse?' encourage the children to use graphophonic cues. When reading the line *Lamb went to the* – a child suggests 'Bull' and another suggests 'Rabbit'. Michael confirms the latter suggestion but then directs the children to go back and reread to check. 'It fits. It fits. Let's have a look and see if we're right.' This encourages the children to use syntactic (structure) and semantic (meaning) cues, and shows the role of prediction in the reading process.

Michael has masked a number of words and when a child attempts to lift the card covering a given word, Michael says, 'I'm not going to show you that yet.' Michael is controlling the removal of the cards, allowing others time to make their own predictions about the hidden word. For instance, the search for the label for a baby horse reveals a number of possibilities. Reading in this way is an enjoyable shared experience in which the class as a group explores the nature of language and the world of books, as well as what reading is and how the reading process works. This occurs with both fictional and factual texts.

TALKING ABOUT FACTUAL TEXTS

Young children want to discover new knowledge and have a passion for information about the world. This passion is fostered from the outset by the inclusion of factual texts on the bookshelf. Michael finds that many of his Preps are drawn to factual texts, particularly those about animals. Good factual texts with clear labelled photographs, such as *Animal Clues*, or others written to encourage inquiry, such as *I Spy*, spark interest and are read and discussed in shared situations and individually during DEAR time.

As a way of demonstrating some of the differences between fictional and factual texts, Michael highlights the different ways that they can be read. Often children think that all books should be read from cover to cover. However, by using factual big books and pointing out locational devices such as table of contents, Michael shows the children that factual texts can be read from various starting points.

Some of the questions used to highlight the differences between fictional and factual texts include:

Predictions:
>What kind of book is this?
>How do you know?
>What kinds of information do you expect to find?
>What kinds of illustrations do you expect to find?

Beginning to read:
>Where can we begin reading this book?
>How else can I read this book?
>What choices do I have? How do you know?

Reading the text:
>What do the headings and subheadings tell me?
>What parts of the book help me find information?
>How do I read the diagrams? (or maps, graphs, timelines)

Locational devices:
>What is the table of contents for? When and how do I use this?
>What do the numbers mean?
>Why are the pages numbered?
>What is the index for? When and how do I use this?
>What do the numbers mean?
>What is the glossary for? When and how do I use this?
>Do all information books have contents, indexes and/or glossaries? Why? Why not?

Thinking about the book:
>Why did the author write the book?
>Whom did the author write the book for?
>Why were the illustrations done in a particular way?

Comparing factual texts with stories:
>How do I read a story? Why?
>(Look at an example such as *Who Will Be My Mother?*)
>Do we read information books or true books in the same way as stories? Why? Why not?
>What things do information books have that storybooks don't?
>What things do storybooks have that information books don't?
>Why are they different?

STARTING OFF WITH FACTUAL TEXTS

STRATEGIES IN COMPARISON
Much time is spent on highlighting the differences between fictional and factual texts. Some of the ways in which this occurs include:
- Making the differences clear through regular teacher talk and demonstration, such as by using the questions above;
- Sorting books into groups: *True, Not True*;

Children compare fictional and factual texts through sorting and predicting activities.

- Guessing from the front cover whether a book will be true or not. Discussing the clues that are used to make such predictions;
- After DEAR time asking children to share what they have read, whether the books were true or not, and how they know this, as well as how they went about reading their books.

READING AND WRITING FACTUAL TEXTS

As the year progresses and the children feel more confident about experimenting with writing and reading, Michael provides numerous opportunities for the children to explore a range of factual genres in more explicit ways.

LET'S GO SHOPPING!

In term 4 much time was spent looking at procedural writing, mostly within an inquiry-based unit of work about shopping. Michael briefly outlines the learning sequence that occurred.

Social education focus

Unit: Shopping
Focus question:
- What range of shops is available to us?

Contributing questions:
- What do shops sell?
- Who works in shops?
- How do I get money to buy items from shops?
- What do I need to buy?
- What do I want to buy?

Language focus

Genre: Procedural
- What is a 'how to'?
- What kinds of information does a 'how to' provide?
- How is this written?
- What helps us find what we want to read in 'how to' books?

INITIAL UNDERSTANDINGS

In order to find out what the children knew about shops, each child was asked to suggest a shop that we might find when we went to the local shopping centre.

A class discussion followed and I recorded what the children knew about shopping. Their initial statements included:

> Shops sell things.
> I go shopping with Mum.
> I buy lollies at the shop.
> McDonalds is like a shop.

STARTING OFF WITH FACTUAL TEXTS

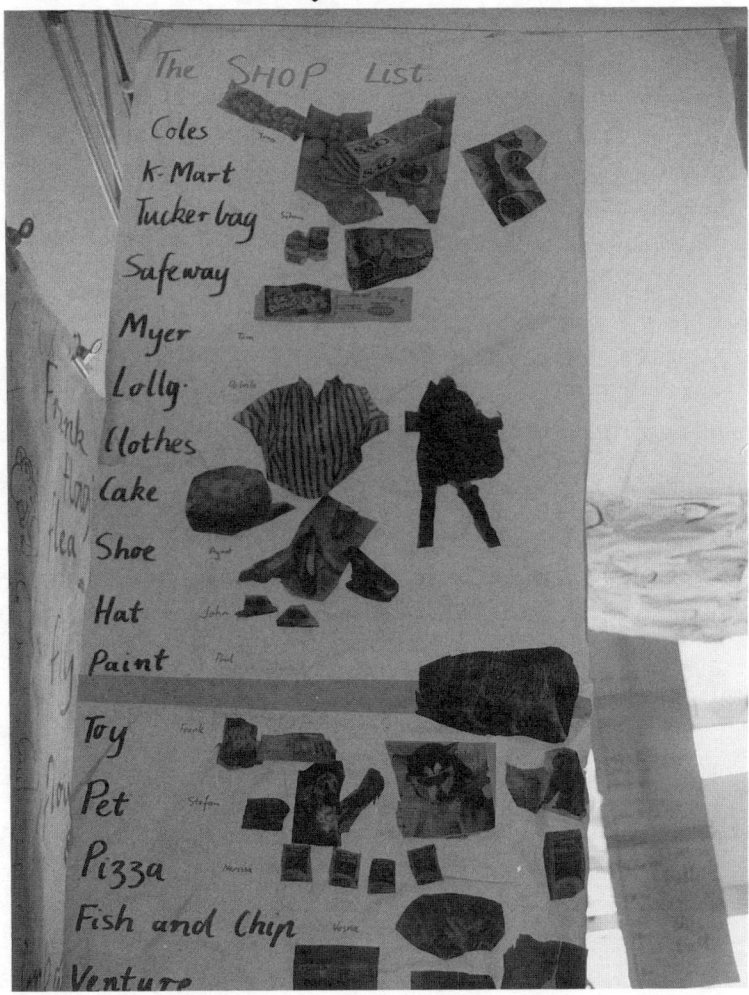

Each child suggested a shop that might be found in the local shopping centre.

BUILDING CONTENT

We visited the local shops. First of all we went to the bank to withdraw the necessary money. Most children had little understanding of this as shown by the comment made by one child: 'Just get the money out of the wall.'

The patient bank staff allowed us to examine the bank forms and I explained the procedure and then demonstrated it. With money in hand we headed off to the shops to make our purchases. We had planned these the day before, and made shopping lists.

The purpose of the shopping expedition was to buy items for a class lunch. Before setting off on our expedition, the children had stipulated that the lunch should have:
- salad with meat or tuna
- seeds in the bread
- fruit

A MATTER OF FACT

A shopping list was compiled, based on the class's requirements.

We had then compiled a shopping list.

We split into small groups (fortunately we had additional staff) and each group purchased the items on their list. When we all returned to school we shared our items stating:
- the name of the item
- the cost
- the shop in which it was purchased.

Then we set about making our lunch. This was a perfect opportunity to demonstrate the various terms that explain how we prepare food such as dicing, grating, buttering and chopping. The talk that accompanied this activity provided terms that would be valuable in later writing.

EXPLICIT TEACHING

After our lunch I demonstrated how to write a procedural text and we wrote on a large piece of paper 'How to make a healthy lunch'.

STARTING OFF WITH FACTUAL TEXTS

Discussion points included:
- listing the ingredients required
- using a numbering system to show the steps
- the importance of an accurate sequence
- the need for clear, brief instructions
- the need for appropriate terms (such as cut, slice, mix)
- the importance of proofreading before giving the instructions to a reader

Many cooking experiences followed our shopping expedition. After our class lunch we read *Kids in the Kitchen*, looking at the recipes for content but also for the way in which they were set out with headings for ingredients (what you need) and for the method (what to do). We discussed the format and purpose of locational devices, such as table of contents, and other elements such as the glossary.

JOINT TEXT CONSTRUCTION

Many activities followed in which we wrote collectively in small groups and/or as a whole class. These included:
- listing the main shops from the shopping centre;
- cutting out pictures depicting items sold.

(These were compared with the initial statements about shopping. We added other shops, such as the hardware shop, to our list.)

Many activities involving joint text construction followed the shopping expedition.

- working in small groups, each with a given number of shops. The children listed the items sold at each shop. Then this was collated onto a chart;
- discussing the notion of being without money. This was new to many children. The children suggested a range of possibilities.

Children suggested a range of possiblities for coping without money.

At this time we were also reading some traditional stories and decided to make a Hansel and Gretel house cake. This provided another opportunity to look at shopping and to consider procedural texts. Again a shopping list was compiled and the necessary shopping was done. Once we had completed (and eaten) the house together we formed small groups and each group member was given a role. We used the roles of leader, writer, reporter, proofreader, timer and materials officer. Each group set about writing a procedural text outlining how to make a Hansel and Gretel house cake.

The instructions are listed using a numbering system which had been discussed previously. A heading 'How to make a Hansel and Gretel house' makes the purpose of the writing clear.

STARTING OFF WITH FACTUAL TEXTS

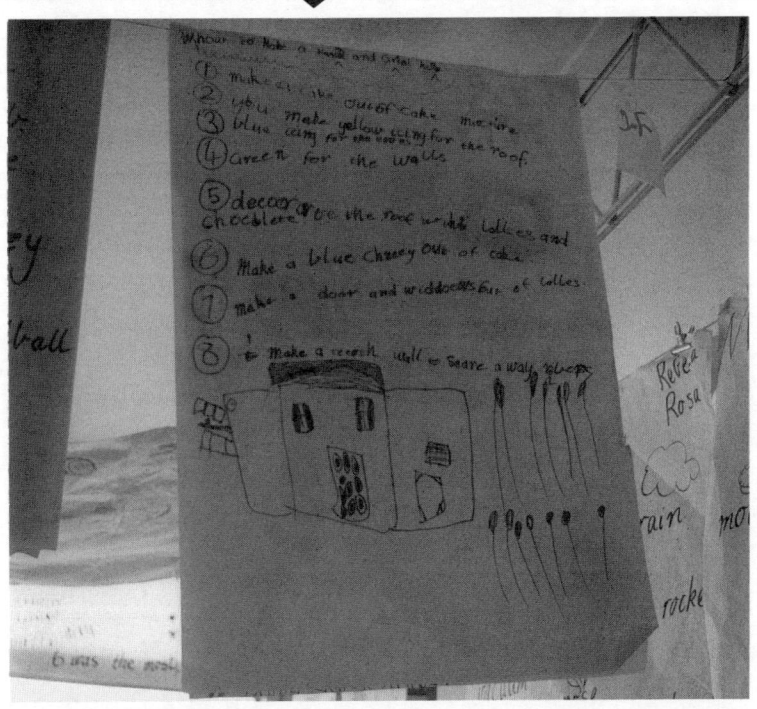

Each group wrote a procedural text on how the make a Hansel and Gretal house cake.

This group drew and listed the required ingredients before writing the instructions, and they outlined the steps in the sequence using a numbering system. The inclusion of ingredients had not been made explicit by my earlier example but the children had taken the idea from their reading of *Kids in the Kitchen*. The children were using their reading experiences in their writing.

INDEPENDENT TEXT CONSTRUCTION

The children have many regular opportunities to write freely on self-selected topics and in any genre that they choose. As their experiences with a range of texts grows, they start to broaden their own writing.

Towards the end of the year it became evident that instances of explicit teaching about a particular genre were being transferred to the children's own writing. An example of where knowledge of procedural texts was used in free choice writing can be found in Naomi's writing. From a range of cooking experiences and the work on shopping, an interest in planting was sparked when the class discussed the origins of items from the greengrocer. Naomi decided to plant beans. She wrote a procedural text outlining how to plant a bean.

---

how to Pelant a been.

① Tauke a Pot.

② put some dirt in the Pot.

③ psh a been in the dirt

④ Cover the seed with dirt

⑤ Water it well evry day

⑥ good luck.

STARTING OFF WITH FACTUAL TEXTS

AN EMPHASIS ON BUILDING CONTENT

A long time is spent on building content and on constructing texts jointly. This is vital; writing for a particular purpose is very difficult unless the content is known and understood. This shared knowledge enables the class to write together on a given topic: they are learning content and gaining understandings about the particular genre simultaneously.

TIME FOR PLAY

There are opportunities for play and experimentation so that experiences can be relived. During the shopping unit, time to play shop was provided regularly and the children relived their experiences as they took turns playing shopkeeper and customers.

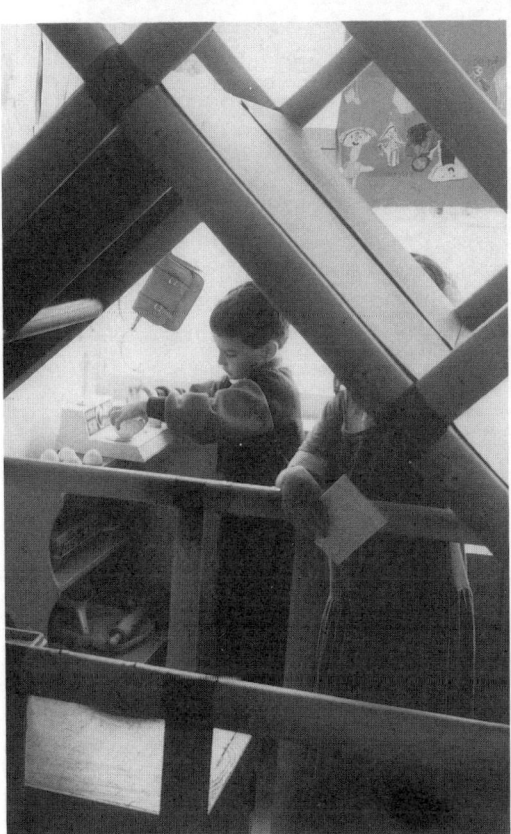
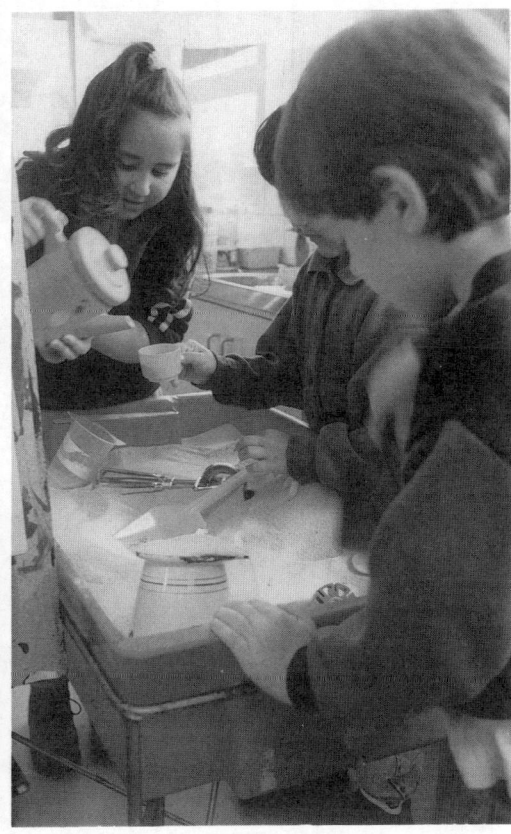

The home corner allowed children to play at cooking.

A group busily washes up from their cooking game.

I see such play as an essential aspect of any unit.

As well as regular free choice writing, opportunity for regular free choice reading (in DEAR, with a cross-age partner, a peer and/or a teacher) is an important part of the daily program.

Regular free choice reading is part of the daily program. This pair reads the class book *Earthworms* together during a quiet moment.

Such strategies pave the way for learning about how texts work.

OVERVIEW OF THE YEAR: FACTUAL GENRES

A range of factual genres have been made explicit over the year. Michael planned for this by constructing an overview of the year. Figure 3.2 highlights a main genre for each term, but there was constant reference to other genres. Although the report genre was made explicit in term 3, the class had read reports before this and continued to do so throughout the year.

STARTING OFF WITH FACTUAL TEXTS

Term	Content/focus	Genre
1	Me My Family	Recount
2	The Farm	Description
3	Earthworms Zoo Animals	Report Report Description
4	Shopping Christmas	Procedural Review of main genres

Figure 3.2 An overview of the factual genres that have been made explicit during the year.

4
TAKING UP NEW CHALLENGES

A Case Study from a Year 2/3 Classroom

◆

Within my own Year 2/3 class there was an enormous range of abilities and interests. All children wrote daily ranging from strings of letters to competent, cohesive pieces of work. Some children were reading short novels, whilst others were just beginning to take an interest in the words on a page. With such a range of abilities, a number of ethnic backgrounds and a wide variety of interests, my challenge was to provide each child with appropriate opportunities to foster language development.

APPROACHES TO LANGUAGE LEARNING

I believe in a holistic approach to language learning, where language is learnt, not by pulling it apart and concentrating on discrete skills, but by using language for meaningful purposes involving the four modes.

Over the year, a number of inquiry-based units of work, drawing on other curriculum areas such as science, social education and health, are devised. The literacy demands of other curriculum areas create opportunities for language learning in authentic contexts, and this involves exposing children to a wide range of written texts, particularly factual texts. For instance, when my Year 2/3 class worked on a unit about food, we looked at procedural texts. After spending time cooking, using a number of recipe books and enjoying our culinary pursuits, we decided to write our own cookbook. This was a way to learn more about food and about procedural texts. A typical 'session' (about an hour and a half) looked like this:

UNIT: Food	LITERACY FOCUS: Procedural texts
Introduction: (10-15 minutes)	Teacher input: read *Let's Cook*. Discuss the format used: what you need and what to do. **(Text demonstration or explicit teaching)**
Focused text exploration: (20-30 minutes)	Children write a favourite recipe using the structure discussed in the introduction. Editing groups are formed where needed. **(Joint text construction)**
Independent writing pursuits: (30 minutes)	Children follow up their own writing pursuits. These may not necessarily relate to the unit being studied. For instance, Nita could continue to write her report about fashion, while Vulcan might write his description of various foodstuffs for his mystery food book. **(Independent text construction)**
	(Teacher engages in **roving** conferences with individuals and **group** conferences as a need is generated.)
Share time: (10-15 minutes)	Whole class share their successes of the session. Any problems are aired and solutions suggested. As the year progresses this time becomes more child than teacher directed.

Figure 4.1 A typical class session of about 1½ hours.

CHOICE

As well as providing set reading and writing tasks, I allow children to choose a selection of writing tasks and of reading material and related tasks to encourage independent decision making and to ensure that children are actively engaged in their language development. For these reasons, part of the session was opened up for broader reading and writing not necessarily related to the unit focus, allowing children to select their own content and the genre used. Children often used genres that had been previously looked at in class.

Daily free reading time (USSR) allowed children to read beyond the focus of the unit being studied.

PREDICTABLE ROUTINES

In my Year 2/3 class, USSR was always held at a specific time of the day (after morning recess) so that the children knew what to do when they came in and wasted no time in settling into the reading material of their choice. Such predictable routines give children a sense of security, so that they could prepare for their day. 'Structure helps them realize their possibilities and assume control of their forward direction.' (Hansen 1987, p.13)

CO-OPERATIVE LEARNING

Co-operation was expected and encouraged. A range of groupings were used throughout the day so that children had opportunities to work in a variety of ways: whole class, small group, paired and individual situations. Such groupings occurred in both formal and informal ways. Informal groups often occurred as the need arose. For instance, when writing our class cookbook and examining *Let's Cook*, the children decided that we should include a table of contents and an index. The table of contents was drafted as a whole class, as everyone needed to contribute their recipe. However, a small group later worked on the draft, organising the recipes according to food type. In sharetime the group reported back to the whole class. A final editing group proofread the recipes, while a publishing group had the task of compiling the book.

The emphasis on class 'experts', a system where each child was known for some area of expertise, encouraged children to help each other and also reinforced the notion that everyone has something to offer. For instance, when planning the index for our cookbook, Luke showed the class what he knew as he was the only one at the time who had written an index before. As the task was too difficult to perform as a whole group, he worked with two interested children, sharing his knowledge.

Co-operative or collaborative learning strategies (as opposed to competition) enhance learning. Hill and Hill (1990) cite a number of current studies indicating that co-operative learning experiences promote higher achievement in academic learning. Such strategies, which focus upon learning with others, promote the development of thinking skills, make learning enjoyable, develop leadership skills, foster positive attitudes, enhance self-esteem and encourage a sense of belonging or group cohesion.

TALK

Talking or conferencing with adults or peers about reading and writing was an important component of the school day. The importance of talking (and listening) was constantly reinforced, especially for children for whom English was their second language. For example, when

Vulcan read his newly published book, *My ABC Book*, the class gave him a great deal of positive feedback.

> *Vulcan read.*
> *Audience laughed and applauded.*
> **Mick:** That was grouse!
> **Kate:** Funny. Real funny.
> **Mick:** Did you do a blurb?
> **Vulcan:** I was going to do a blurb. I was going to. . . I have done three books and they're called *My ABC Book, My New Clothes* and *The Cat in the Hat.*
> **Luke:** You could write. . . Hi! My name is Vulcan. And I. . . How old are you Vulcan?
> **Vulcan:** Seven.
> **Luke:** Hi! My name is Vulcan and I'm seven years old and I done a counting book. . . an ABC book and it took me a long while to do it or something.

As well as gaining recognition for his achievement, the comments from his peers, especially Luke, encouraged Vulcan to extend himself further by adding a blurb.

Wells (1986) found that listening and talking about reading and writing is vital to the extension of children's experience beyond the limits of their surroundings. Collaborative talk is an important element of co-operative learning strategies and promotes the development of a community of learners in which learning is shared.

ASSESSMENT

Assessment was ongoing so that planning could develop and change according to the perceived needs and interests of the children. Methods of assessment included observation, updating class charts of the children's writing pursuits and their current reading (reading reckoner), hearing children read and talking with them about their reading and writing. The children were encouraged to assess themselves by regularly updating their writing folders and examining their progress, and by sharing their progress at share time. The most valuable source of information lay in the children's attitudes to reading and writing.

A COMMUNITY OF READERS AND WRITERS

The promotion of 'a community of readers and writers' (Hansen 1987) is crucial to language learning. This was promoted in many ways, such as by the celebration of successes which was largely the function of share time. The expectation that the children would do their best was made clear. Our class motto, 'You'll never know if you don't have a go,' encouraged children to take risks within the security of the classroom environment. The seeking and mastery of new challenges, no matter how large or small, were shared.

The celebration occurred in a number of ways, such as a round of applause, a loud cheer, a smile, a few words of praise or by displaying a product. The celebration varied from child to child. For instance, when James successfully wrote his name, it was time to celebrate and he was met with applause and then proceeded to share his success with other teachers in the school. When Lisa worked out how to do a glossary, her name was added to the our expert list and she was noted as having expertise in this area.

PHYSICAL ASPECTS

Our classroom was part of an open-plan building where few walls divided one classroom from the next. The unit that housed my class of 2/3 children also accommodated a group of Year 3/4 children. Each class used half of the unit, which was equivalent to two classrooms and one reading room each.

The room plan is provided because the physical set-up is vital to the language learning that can be promoted and also because the explanation of such a set-up shows how the classroom operated.

INTERACTION

There was ample floor space, providing areas for whole class discussions and group conferences. The tables were placed in groups to encourage interaction, as 'proximity promotes interaction.' (Hansen 1987, p.75) If children are to be encouraged to talk about their work and to provide each other with feedback, they need access to each other.

QUIET AREAS

Children need to be able to choose to work in a quiet place. Therefore a quiet area, which could be used for more solitary activities, was set up and draped with fabric to create an illusion of privacy. The children used the quiet area when they wished to read in the comfort of the bean bags and cushions. The furniture was well spaced so that children could move without disturbing others.

DISPLAY OF RESOURCES

There was sufficient space for many displays and for each child to have an individual display section, which encouraged them to share in the creation of an interesting and dynamic classroom environment. Long-term displays, such as our 'expert area' section, our daily notice board and our new publications, could be maintained and updated, and there was also room for short-term displays. There were book displays, such as our factual texts, poetry, novels and picture story books, and there were also art displays, a science area and a mathematics trolley. There

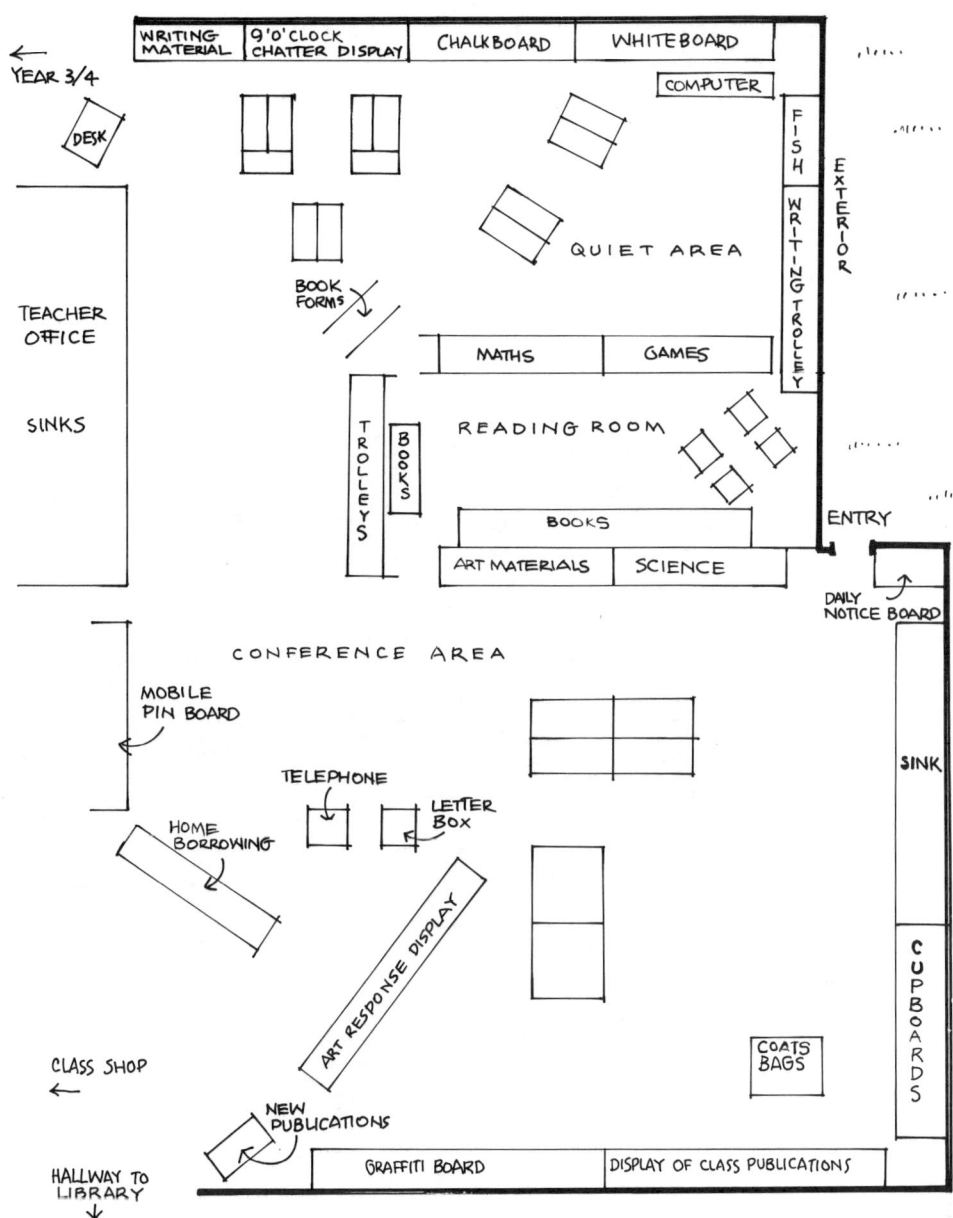

Figure 4.2 The physical layout of Pam's Year 2/3 classroom

was room for a shop, a post office, a graffiti board and a phone box, to encourage talking, listening, reading and writing.

Resources in the room were clearly labelled and accessible to the children, so that they could operate independently and proceed with a range of tasks without needing permission or physical assistance from anyone else. There was a writing trolley and a table of art materials, which were in constant use. A computer was placed in a central position to enable regular use and constant supervision, and so that help for users could be readily given (from computer 'experts' or the teacher).

INTRODUCING NITA: A CASE STUDY

We can learn much about how a child learns as well as the way in which a class operates by closely monitoring the development of an individual child. The following case study shows how using a range of text genres, especially factual texts, encourages literacy growth by extending children's writing options.

Nita's writing options are enhanced through exploration of commercial and class texts.

Nita's blurb was written in September to accompany her rhyme 'Spaghetti Bolognaise'. Nita clearly knows the function of a blurb, which had been explored throughout the year through commercial texts and our own class texts.

There is evidence of some revision, especially in the use of commas, to list her family members. When revising, Nita would firstly read to check content and continually asked herself and/or others 'Does it make sense?' Then she would address some of the surface features, such as the use of commas, in follow-up conferences after initial conferences related to the content. These follow-up conferences usually focused on one feature at a time. Concentrating on all the surface

> Hi, ~~my~~ my nave is Nita I am ~~eight~~ years old ~~I am~~ Im nine in October I have published 2 books in 1989 they are riddles in MAY and Nita's HOLIDAY DIARY in September I ~~Hope you~~ I have a mum, ~~and~~ a dad, 2 brothers, ~~I a~~ 1 sister, and myself ~~Hope~~ and we ~~$~~ are very happy Hope you engoyed my book and see you round

features at once seemed to threaten Nita's confidence and detracted from the writing, as well as often being too much to deal with in one conference.

The blurb reveals an air of confidence and a sense of pride in the achievements made so far in the year. The achievements went well beyond the publication of a number of texts. The following letter, written at the end of the year, showed extensive use of a number of terms relating to many features of factual texts.

> Dear Elane,
> The books you lent~~ed~~ us were GREAT. I liked ~~A What~~ Mce Mice I lernt how to ~~to~~ write a table of Contents, ~~the~~ blurb an index and a © that means no one can copy your book. I have put a © on my fashion book and a blurb an index and a table of contents It was great meeting you Merry Christmas and happy new year,
> Love from Nita

Nita's understanding of these terms and her ability to put them into practice, which developed over the year, is demonstrated in her writing.

NITA: THE WRITER

When considering Nita's writing development Smith's term 'reading like a writer' is appropriate (Smith 1983). As the year progressed and she became increasingly familiar with a wide range of texts, Nita began searching for ideas for her own writing as she was reading. Initially, however, her writing ideas were solidly based in her day-to-day experiences.

In the early part of the year, Nita's writing was prolific but she was not interested in reworking pieces with a view to publication. The early samples from her first draft folder revealed a number of recounts related mainly to school experiences. The following narrative piece, written in February, was revised along the way, but this process was apparently burdensome for Nita, and she neglected to complete the piece.

[Handwritten draft titled "Kathryns Flying shoe":]

Nell it all started at School. Kathryn was spinning around and around And her shoe skidded along the ground. Then I slid along the ground and picked it up and I pretended to throw it up so I threw it up into the air well we didnt see Anything

---

Kathryn's Flying Shoe reveals a delight in retelling events in order to create a humorous piece of writing. Nita attended to the spelling as she wrote, and had some strategies for finding the correct spelling.

READING LIKE A WRITER

In June/July, motivated by Spike Milligan's poem 'The ABC' in *More, Read It Again Please*, Nita began to write her own ABC book. The title of her piece *ABC, It's Easy As One, Two, Three* reveals her interest in rhyme and the effect of focusing on various genres and making reading/writing connections. There is evidence of revision, not so much of surface features but of content. It seems that by this stage in the year she had learnt to focus on the content first so that the meaning could be clearly expressed. Nita wrote out the alphabet in a simple

TAKING UP NEW CHALLENGES

way, (a is for arrow) and then reread the piece and extended each entry to make it more detailed and interesting. However, Nita did not choose to publish this piece. It seemed that purpose and pleasure were derived from the writing, but that her interest was not sufficient to engage her further in the subsequent conferences and the revision necessary for publication.

> A BC ~~A BC~~ ~~Just for mama~~ A BC it's easy as one two three
>
> rais for arrow that I can shoot ~~threw~~ an apple
>
> B is for Bear that rides on a bike
>
> C is for Crown with Dimonds around ~~C is for Cat we have~~
>
> D is for dog that barks Down the street
>
> E is for Envlope ~~lat we~~ is stidey
>
> F is for frog that sits on a footy
>
> G is for gun that chats stor at voters
>
> H is for Horse that weres ~~Horse~~ Honches hat
>
> I is for irden that ions our clothes
>
> J is for Jack in the Box that Jumps Usand Down
>
> K is for Koala that flies a kite
>
> L is for lizard thrt lies Under a lamp
>
> M is for mop ~~to~~ that mops the floor
>
> N is for ~~a~~ necklace that nita weres
>
> O is for oven that opens and shuts

Nita's interest in writing did not extend beyond writing sessions until third term. Her holiday diary, which was written and published in July, represented a major breakthrough, and was motivated by her interest in Robin Klein's book *Penny Pollard's Diary* which she had selected for her own class reading. The idea for the diary itself also came from our own class diaries and also, as Nita put it, '. . . from my holidays . . . I wanted to do a book about what I done in the holidays.' Apparently, she had been thinking about her next piece of writing and had used a variety of sources for ideas. It was not until this piece had been written that Nita decided that she would go on to the publication stage of the writing process. The diary consisted of two main parts so Nita wrote a table of contents for the reader's information.

> Contents
> 1. The Zoo 1
> ~~2~~ 2 Luna Park 6.

The inclusion of a table of contents reveals the impact of explicit teaching which highlighted this as a useful feature, particularly in factual texts. For instance, in the joint construction of our fish book, we discussed the table of contents from a number of texts, especially *Mice, Mice, Mice*. I recorded details, such as chapter headings and page numbers on a chart as the children contributed details about the chapters they had written.

Although Nita's table of contents is simple, it is composed of chapter headings and page numbers. Nita used a number of resources for her writing, such as class charts, class publications, other children and commercial texts. She was a fairly competent and confident reader and so could independently consult the available texts. She frequently consulted *Mice, Mice, Mice* which had been a major focus in class activities.

THE IMPACT OF FEEDBACK

Sharing this book provided Nita with positive feedback. She received credit for including a table of contents and for making use of the available resources. When a classmate suggested that she might have included an index, Nita showed her understanding of indexes by replying that an index would have been inappropriate '. . .because . . .there's really only two things that it's really about in there.' She included a copyright sign and was clear about its purpose. This had been an aspect of publishing that had become explicit through our use of the commercial texts and in our own publishing. Later, in August, when another classmate Vulcan shared his *Cat in the Hat* book, Nita recommended that he might have used a copyright sign '. . .so no one could copy it.'

Nita's classmates were very interested in the way she had used fabric, ribbon and lace to decorate the diary, and how she had used pressed flowers instead of illustrations, which she thought more appropriate for a diary. They were also interested in the way she ended her diary with a series of postscripts to provide extra information for the reader. The other children did not understand the purpose of postscripts and Nita explained it to them. This gave her an expertise status, which was recorded on our list of class experts.

Praise was always given when a child attempted a new challenge in writing. New challenges were highlighted to further encourage children to take risks and to extend themselves. Nita attempted to set herself a number of new challenges in her diary and received encouragement from me and from her peers.

A BLEND OF TEXT GENRES

The holiday diary ultimately represented a blend of the narrative and the recount genres. Nita admitted to this mixing of recollected events and fiction when she shared her favourite part. She said she liked the part she had written '. . .about chasing Casey in the park.' When asked

TAKING UP NEW CHALLENGES

> Nita's Holiday diary   The Zoo
>
> On ~~Friday~~ Monday I went to the ~~Zoo~~ but first I went to Sims to get a pair of reebok. When we got there I tried on two (pairs) of Reebok first I tried on a pair of boots ~~Back~~ they were Blue and white. Then I tried on a pair of grey ~~and~~ and white ones.

why this was her favourite part, Nita said, 'Because I made it up and it sounded like they were really doing it right now.' This statement revealed her growing interest in and understanding of the difference between story and truth, an understanding that was demonstrated when Nita explained to me the difference between storybooks and information books. 'Well, storybooks. . . most of them aren't true and information books are true and they're telling you something.' The inclusion of fictional elements reveals Nita's growing sense of audience. Her purpose in the piece was not merely to inform but also to entertain.

NOTHING SUCCEEDS LIKE SUCCESS

Motivated by the successes of her holiday diary, Nita began to spend a great deal of her time writing. She wrote at home and at school. One morning she shared a rhyme 'Spaghetti Bolognaise', which she had composed the night before at home. The rhyme, which was written on her father's invoice book, shows Nita's delight in playing with language, and is included because it demonstrates her enthusiasm for writing (see page 70).

A few months earlier I had established a daily notice board as a means of conveying news about the day's events, and also to encourage reading and writing for yet another purpose. Writing the daily message was my task until Nita asked me one morning if she could write up a message. As a result, she took over my role and soon other children wanted to take their turn. This shows her interest in writing, as well as revealing the impact of peer writing in motivating others to write.

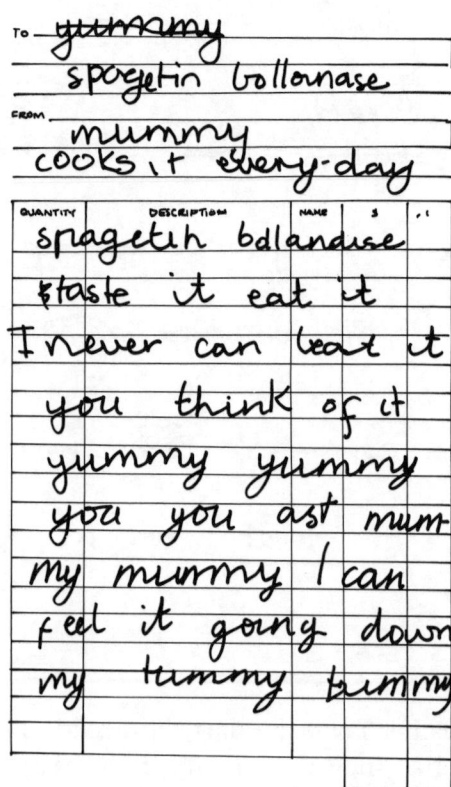

Her desire to write was often shown by her comments in class. For instance, when I mentioned that the children could move onto their own writing, her enthusiastic response was 'Oh, grouse,' or 'Yesss!'

OUR SPELLING EXPERT

The writing samples shown so far reveal some competence in spelling, and Nita became known as one of the class spelling experts. She was often consulted by other children for help with spelling. She followed up her role as 'spelling expert' by checking the daily notice board for spelling. This status as an expert further increased her confidence and interest in writing.

Nita had been involved in writing procedural texts, particularly our fish book. Such experiences clearly influenced her writing decisions, as Nita's next major piece of writing was a procedural text entitled *Fashion*.

Whilst structural information about factual writing, such as how to set out an index, came from jointly constructed class texts, the ideas for the topic came from an advertisement and, indirectly, from her sister who had made the comment about an item of clothing, 'That's not in fashion.' Nita explained, 'And I thought I can do a fashion book.' Nita was constantly on the alert for ideas to use in her writing. She used information from books borrowed from our Year 5/6 friends, who had helped us with our *Fish, Fish, Fish* book.

Nita's fashion book showed the use of chapter headings and page numbers, which were assembled into a table of contents. This, like the inclusion of a blurb, was now a standard part of her writing. The new challenge for Nita was writing a procedural text and including an index.

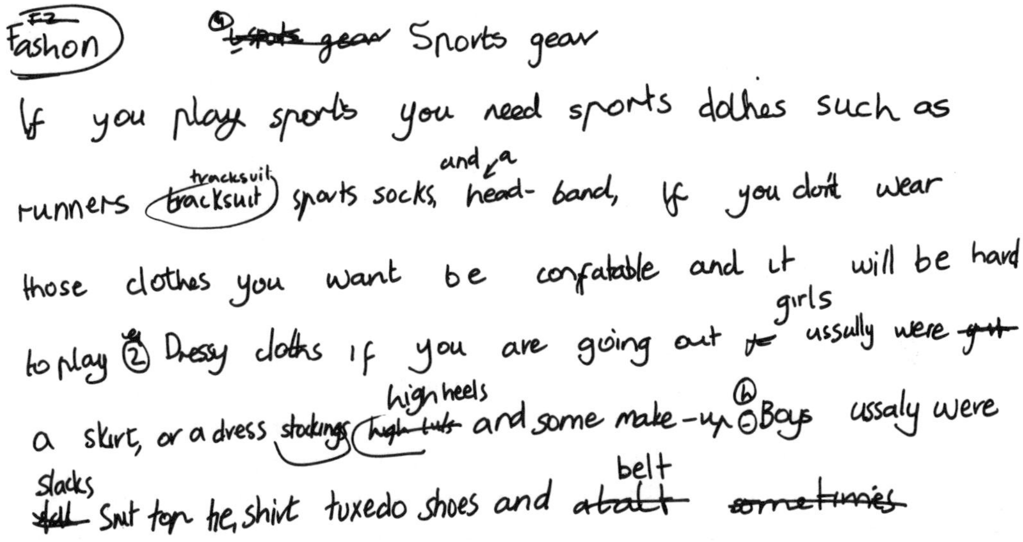

[Handwritten draft:]

Fashion

① ~~Sports gear~~ Sports gear

If you play sports you need sports clothes such as runners (tracksuit) sports socks, and a head-band. If you don't wear those clothes you want be confatable and it will be hard to play ② Dressy cloths if you are going out girls ussually were a skirt, or a dress, stockings (high heels) and some make-up ⑥ Boys ussaly were slacks Suit top tie, shirt tuxedo shoes and belt ~~sometimes~~

Nita writes with the reader in mind and supplies direct information about a number of aspects of fashion for both boys and girls. The chapter headings are included in the body of the text in this draft, and the numbers related to the intended pagination. These numbers were added when the index was being planned.

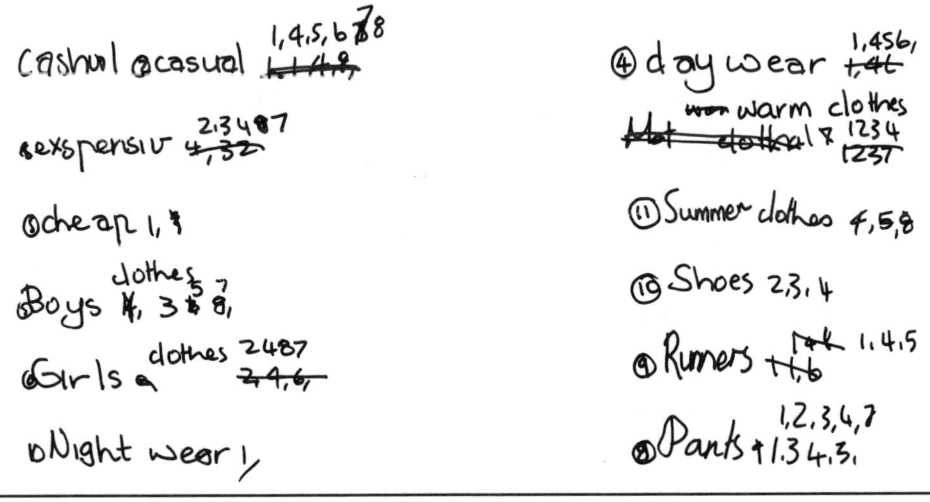

[Handwritten index:]

cashul ① casual 1,4,5,6,7,8

⑤ xspensiv 2,3,4,7

① cheap 1,8

⑤ Boys clothes 4,3,7,8

⑥ Girls clothes 2,4,8,7

⓪ Night wear 1,

④ day wear 1,4,5,6,

warm clothes 1,2,3,4, 1,2,3,7

⑪ Summer clothes 4,5,8

⑩ Shoes 2,3,4

⑨ Runners 1,4,5

⑧ Pants 1,2,3,4,7

The numbers on the left-hand side of the fashion topics show how they would be placed when written in alphabetical order. Nita used classroom resources to help her work out how to create an index. 'For the index I used *What's My Hobby?*' Towards the end of the year, when we reviewed the usefulness of factual texts which had been the basis for much of our class program, Nita highlighted the impact of the jointly constructed class book about fish. She told how *Mice, Mice, Mice* had led to the writing of *Fish, Fish, Fish,* and how she had learnt about 'the table of contents and [I] learnt how to do an index' as a result.

After sharing her fashion book with the class, Nita was often consulted by other children about writing indexes. This became another area of expertise, which gave her positive feedback. Further feedback came when the children's publications were displayed to a group of teachers at another school who were interested in factual writing. Nita had worked hard to have her book ready. This had provided her with a wider audience, which she eagerly sought. She was praised for her efforts, both within and outside our school.

Nita was frequently called upon to act as an editor in preparing writing for publication. For instance, when writing the food glossary for our class cookbook, Nita worked as an editor with two others and continually asked 'Does this make sense?' The role of an editor in the writing process had been made explicit through our work with Year 5/6 and through a number of other tasks. The following report was written by Nita, after a class excursion to Horsebend Farm.

~~Rob~~ {Farm Report}

Animal DOG
Reporter Nita
Editor Kate

A male dog is called a dog. The female people call it a bitch. And a little dog is called a pup. Hey do you that a group of DOGS is called a kennel ~~Its~~ Its probabaly named after where they sleep because they sleep in kennels.

It's = it is

| P | r | o | b | a | b | l | y |

Nita was the reporter and Kate was her editor for this report. The use of the correct terminology for these writing roles is evident. When I asked Nita to explain the role of an editor, she replied 'They need to proofread it. . . Check it and see if it makes sense.' Teacher talk and classroom interaction, as well as the exploration and implementation of these roles, demonstrated the purpose of such terminology.

Nita was extending her own repertoire of terms, which she employed to talk about the processes and roles involved in writing, as well as in discussing her own writing and that of others. The report reveals the use of Clay's (1985) letter box strategy for attending to spelling, which Nita found useful.

COLLATING INFORMATION

I had used the tables in *What Did you Eat Today?* to show the class how to use a table to collect and arrange information, and gave them the opportunity to collate their own information about their eating habits. Nita's simple table, below, represents an innovation on the original text.

Nita then transferred this method of data presentation to her own factual text, *Hidden Houses*. She wanted to collect information about housing, so she interviewed about twelve people, using prepared questions, and then presented the information as a table. She had clearly been influenced by the previous activities, and by factual texts themselves.

A MATTER OF FACT

	The street they live in	Number of the house	Suburbs	Whats the house made of	Color of fence
Vulcan ~~17~~ 21	Kylrram	131	Coolaroo	Bricks	White
Mick ~~8~~ 15	Paisley str	12	Coolaroo	Bricks	brown
Kate ~~10~~ 11	Elm crt	3	Coolaroo	Bricks	back fence Brown
Sally ~~8~~ 19 ✗	Kybram	12	Coolaroo	Bricks	Silver
Miss Green 16	Ingrams road	106	reserch	Timber	Brown

The school year was drawing to a close. Nita set herself the goal of completing her book and worked to self-imposed deadlines. She worked consistently, writing up the information into a report which shows a clear understanding of the nature of the task.

~~Miss Earth~~ Mysteryperson No 1
Kate lives at 13 Elm Court Coolaroo. Her house is made of bricks The color of her fence is brown. ~~Miss Peters~~ ~~Lisa~~ lives at 60 Primrose Crt in Essendon ~~Her fence is brown~~ ~~and~~ Her house is made ~~of timber and her fence is brown~~. She hasn't got a fence. Mick lives in Paisly Street. The number of the house is 12 he lives in Coolaroo. His house is made of bricks. His ~~house~~ fence is brown.

To make the book interesting, Nita added a guessing element by using a series of mystery house numbers which could be traced back to the inhabitant of each house. This was a strategy that she experienced previously, and Nita knew that it would gain the reader's attention. She tried to give each house a number so that she could organise the information and provide an element of prediction.

TAKING UP NEW CHALLENGES

①kathryn 4/12/89
⑥Sally Mystery Number 3
  ④Pam Mystery Number 60
Mrs Green Mystery Number 10
  ②Lisa Mystery Number 106
Miss Peters Mystery Number 34
③Mick Mystery Number 125
⑤Ryan

Mystery house No. 3
Mystery 2 house No. 60
Mystery 3 house No. 12
Mystery 4 house No. 106
~~Mystery 5 house No. 34~~
Mystery 5 house No. 125

The task that Nita set for herself provided her with a range of new challenges, especially in data collection and collation. As well, she extended herself to report writing in an inquiry format. She included a title page, providing the publishing details and a copyright sign.

Hidden Houses
Illustrator: Nita
  Author: Nita
Nita's writing Department
  © copy wright

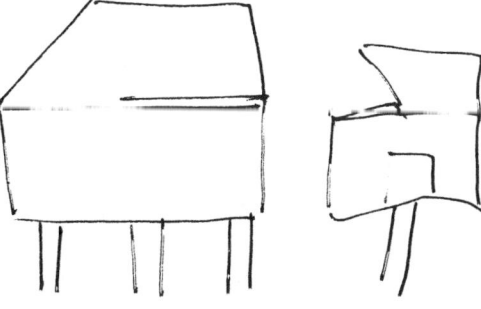

EXPLICIT TEACHING

This final piece of writing for the year further reveals the impact of explicit teaching using factual texts. A number of commercial texts in the report genre and the inquiry mode of writing had been used in the latter part of the year and there had been much interest in these texts. The element of prediction and of surprise attracted the children's attention, and was a regular part of my teaching repertoire. Nita was one of the children in the class who tried out this style of writing, on the basis that it would appeal to the reader. She made the statement, 'I'm going to make a book like that one,' in reference to *What Did You Eat Today?*, an inquiry-based text. Nita was reading like a writer, seeking ideas for her own writing while she read.

Nita had discovered a number of writing options. This understanding was evident when I asked her why we used the term 'writing', rather than the term 'story writing'. Nita replied, 'Because you could do letter writing or information or diary writing.' She knew that writing could take a variety of forms and was not limited to story. She was increasing her text repertoire: she had an increasing number of written texts that she was familiar with and a growing vocabulary of terminology with which to discuss issues related to the writing process. She was also developing a range of strategies in data collection, such as interviewing, and tabulating results. Her writing revealed a growing sense of audience. As her confidence grew, Nita realised that she was a writer and became more aware of the links between reading and writing. Nita was writing like a reader. The positive feedback that Nita received when her achievements were recognised added further impetus to her language growth.

Figure 4.3 shows the links between commercially-produced written texts introduced to the class, the jointly constructed class texts and Nita's independent writing pursuits. The commercially produced texts that were introduced during the latter part of the year are listed and paralleled with the class books made in that time. In order to show the growth of Nita's text repertoire, her independently constructed texts over the whole year are listed.

Nita spent the first half of the year mainly writing narratives, and then moved into factual writing by experimenting with description in her ABC book. She was fascinated by riddle and rhyme, and continued to explore these aspects of narrative. By October, after seeing a number of texts and writing several class books in both the report and procedural text genres, Nita began to add these to her text repertoire. Several parallels can be drawn between the introduction of commercial texts, the writing of class books and Nita's own writing. For instance, the inquiry-based book entitled *What Did You Eat Today?* was introduced and led to exploration with collecting information in tables to compile our own class text of the same name. Using the inquiry format from the commercial and class books, as well as the data collection technique used in class, Nita compiled information about houses into her own book, *Hidden Houses*.

Month	Text demonstration Genre	Title	Jointly constructed texts Genre	Title	Independent text construction: Nita Genre	Title
FEBRUARY					Narrative	Kathryn's Flying Shoe
MARCH					Inquiry/ Narrative	Riddles
APRIL					Recount	The Tired Walk
MAY					Tall Story/ Narrative	Kittens in a Pot
JUNE						
JULY	Rhyme Rhyme Rhyme Rhyme Report	Kangaroo Court Five Little Monkeys More Read it Again, Please Jelly on a Plate Bush Secrets	Rhyme Inquiry/ Description	Five Little Dogs Animal Clues	Description Recount/ Narrative	ABC- It's Easy as 1,2,3. Nita's Holiday Diary
AUGUST	Report Procedural Report	River Red Mice, Mice, Mice What's your Hobby	Report Procedural	What's Your Hobby? Fish, Fish, Fish		
SEPTEMBER	Report Rhyme	Animal Jigsaws Oh, She's Lucky	Report Inquiry/ Description Rhyme	Our Collection of Animal Reports What am I? Oh, She's Lucky	Narrative/ Rhyme	Spaghetti Bolognaise
OCTOBER	Inquiry/ Description Inquiry/ Description Report	Creature Features Hidden animals Food, Glorious, Food	Inquiry/ Description Report Inquiry/ Description	Creature Features The Greatest Grade's News Hidden Animals	Procedural Recount	Fashion A Tassie Trip
NOVEMBER	Procedural Inquiry/ Description Traditional Tale	Let's Cook What Did You Eat Today? Stone Soup	Inquiry/ Description	What Did You Eat Today?	Report	Pandas
DECEMBER	Report Explanation	Lizards Skin, Scales, Feathers and Fur	Procedural	Our Christmas Cookbook	Inquiry/ Description	Hidden Houses

Figure 4.3 Extending Nita's text repertoire

As Nita successfully met new challenges, her confidence grew, sparking off a greater interest in writing and the pursuit of further challenges.

Surface features, such as spelling and punctuation, were attended to in the final part of drafting; interest in and experimentation with new text genres, particularly reports and descriptions written in inquiry formats, is evident; locational devices, such as table of contents and indexes, were incorporated into final publication of factual texts and publication details, such as date and place of publishing, the publisher and copyright, were included.

Month	Title	Genre	Challenge
FEBRUARY	Kathryn's Flying Shoe	Narrative	Ongoing writing Revising: spelling Punctuating: capitals, full stops Publishing

Month	Title	Genre	Challenge
MARCH	Riddles	Inquiry/ Narrative	Humour Question/Answer format Use of question marks Word processing Dedication
APRIL	The Tired Walk	Recount	
MAY	Kittens in a Pot	Tall story	Sense of audience
JUNE	ABC- It's easy as 1,2,3.	Narrative	Audience: infants Innovating on a text: poem
JULY	Nita's Holiday Diary	Narrative/ Recount	Extending length Table of contents Copyright Chapter headings Page numbers Range of publishing media
SEPTEMBER	Spaghetti Bolognaise	Narrative/ Rhyme	Writing at home Blurb
OCTOBER	Fashion	Procedural	Table of contents Blurb Index

Month	Title	Genre	Challenge
NOVEMBER	A Tassie Trip Pandas	Recount Report	Dedication Date of publication Word processing Spelling strategies Newspaper format Writing/publishing at home
DECEMBER	Hidden Houses	Inquiry/ Description	Interviewing Collecting data in grids Frontispiece Publishing company Publication date Shape format

Figure 4.4 An analysis of Nita's independent text construction. The extension of writing challenges can be seen as Nita sought new challenges through independent text construction whilst building on earlier challenges.

CONCLUSIONS

Factual texts have an important role in our classrooms. By working with factual texts in explicit ways and by exposing children to a range of text genres, we can extend their text repertoires and increase their options for writing, allowing children to write for a broad range of purposes.

The case study shows the effect of exposure to a range of text genres on children's writing. By examining Nita's writing pursuits and by asking her about her learning it was clear that the introduction of a range of text genres did affect her writing. She had greater options in her writing choices and in selecting new challenges to pursue, leading to increased confidence and interest in writing and reading.

The children used a wide range of resources — commercial texts, jointly constructed texts, class charts from text demonstrations and texts constructed by peers — and they became familiar with and confident in seeking out such materials. Increased interest in writing and reading meant that they concentrated more on their written texts, spending more time revising and following pieces through to the publication stage. This led to an increased awareness of the roles in the writing process, such as author and editor. The children became interested in looking up publication and copyright details in books and then incorporated these details in their own publications. The use of 'considerate' factual texts for real purposes enabled the children to understand locational devices, such as table of contents and indexes, and to then apply them to their own writing.

The connections between writing and reading became apparent to them, especially when they began to read more widely and started to 'read as writers', searching for ideas for their own writing. When the children began to 'write as readers,' they wrote with a clear purpose in mind and a growing sense of audience.

The children's vocabulary grew, and their interaction became more focused and related to writing tasks at hand. The classroom interaction became very supportive. The capacity to listen constructively to others and to act as a 'critical friend' increased. Peer conferencing and cross-age tutoring, often based on teacher demonstration, provided further support for children's language development. Social skills were extended through collaborative work, and the children became more confident and competent in speaking in front of others and offering assistance to others. A spirit of co-operation and support grew, and a community of talkers, listeners, writers and readers emerged.

5
LITERACY DEMANDS IN A YEAR 6 CLASS

We meet Andrea Johnson's class in the final term of their primary schooling. By this stage the children have explored a range of different types of reading and writing, both fictional and factual, and have many options for their own language use.

BASIC ASSUMPTIONS

The class operates on a number of basic assumptions drawn from Andrea's teaching/learning philosophy.

RESPONSIBLE LEARNERS

Andrea expects her children to be responsible learners. She believes that children learn best when the learning is relevant to them and when they have opportunity to make decisions and choices about their learning. In this way children will have a stake in their learning. Ultimately the responsibility for learning rests with the learner.

Opportunities to make decisions and to act responsibly increase during the school year. A walk into Andrea's class during the final term shows the strength of this philosophy in practice. In one of the literature groups, for instance, Sue was acting as leader and conducting an animated conference about the novel *The Green Wind*. Each group member offered a comment about the book and had information to share about Coolgardie safes, which had been the task negotiated by the group the week before. Each child acted responsibly and contributed with enthusiasm. However, such learning does not occur in a vacuum: much support had been provided during the year and was still not far away if needed.

ORGANISATIONAL STRUCTURES

Andrea encourages the children to be responsible learners, but she does not lose sight of the need to provide ongoing support for the development of such responsibility. In situations like the conference group above, there are organisational structures to support the learning. For instance, the routine of the group work occurs on a regular basis so that the children know when they will have opportunities to share their negotiated tasks. Group leaders, who change over the year, have access to teacher resources. Andrea demonstrates the preparation that occurs for such work and provides access to teacher references supplying discussion starters and ideas for follow-up tasks.

REFLECTION

Boomer (1984) draws attention to the need for teachers to talk openly with students '. . .about why they do what they do, about how they think people learn and about the societal consequences of various behaviours.' (p.122) A lot of time in Andrea's class is spent talking about learning. She actively encourages the children to become aware of their role in their own learning and to support each other by talking and writing constructively about their work.

Time is provided for reflecting on what they have learned and how they learned, such as by setting aside five or ten minutes at the end of the day for a reflective journal entry or for a discussion of the day's events and the learning that occurred.

Children discuss the day's events and the learning that occurred.

LITERACY DEMANDS IN A YEAR 6 CLASS

The children are encouraged to set themselves new challenges by reflecting on and celebrating their successes as well as seeking resolutions for any concerns or problems. Statements often begin with the following:

I learned how to/about...
Things that helped me learn were...
I feel pleased about...
Now I am an expert at...
I feel concerned about...
I need to work on...
Next time I could try...

> 1) I am good at school work, cricket, swimming, running, bat tennis, and volleyball, and Music.
> 2) The things I find difficult are, soccer, and some computer games.
> 3) I (whoul) would like to be better at football, tennis, handwriting, Art, and cricket.
> 4) I think I need to improve in, concentrating, and not talking
> 5) When a teacher collects assessment information about me I think they are interested to know what I need to improve in because then she could teach more of that and less of what I am good at.

CO-OPERATIVE GROUP STRATEGIES

Part of being a responsible learner involves working with others in various ways and taking on a range of roles. Co-operative group strategies are promoted, beginning with work in pairs, and then moving to small groups of 3 or 4 and later to larger groups. The group size depends on the task at hand.

The regular use and rotation of designated roles, such as reporter, scribe, timer, summariser, clarifier (or questioner) and leader, occurred earlier in the year but is no longer necessary. While Andrea ensures that each child learns to operate in different ways and contributes to their group, she also believes that, in reality, roles emerge as group members interact with each other. These roles generally emerge in response to the tasks in which the group is engaged. Group work has now been established to give further opportunity for the children to act responsibly and to have some say in the way in which they contribute. In an effort to keep track of the roles taken, Andrea keeps a simple checklist showing the date when each role is held.

Name	Reporter	Scribe	Timer	Leader	Summariser	Clarifier
Sally	15/3		28/7		5/6	

Regular time for all groups to reflect on and talk about group processes is essential. Peer assessment works well here, as the children realise that it is in their own interests to learn to work well together. At times, the children list 'helps' and 'hinders' to learning. The items under 'hinders' then become challenges or problems to overcome, while the 'helps' are viewed as strengths.

THINK ABOUT YOUR LEARNING!!!!!

HELPS	HINDERS
Encouragement Parents Teachers examples instructions friends time reading (newspapers, books, worksheets) School ask questions People talk to you about it information (surveys, interviews)	time fear friend Embaressment interruption

The benefits of collaborative or co-operative group strategies are apparent:
- children provide each other with support in the form of encouragement and constructive criticism;
- areas of expertise among children are shared as they teach each other various skills as well as what they know;
- a sense of 'community' within the class is fostered as successes are jointly celebrated while challenges or concerns are faced together;
- a sense of responsibility is developed as children take a stake in their learning and see the consequences of their contributions in terms of the group and the whole class as well as for themselves as individuals.

Of course not all work occurs within groups. Responsible learners need to be able to work independently and opportunities for this are incorporated into the classroom program.

AN INTEGRATED CURRICULUM

Concern is shown for the literacy demands within all curriculum areas with particularly strong links between language and mathematics. Knowledge, skills and values are promoted through the investigation of broad topics. Andrea believes that this approach promotes active learning. This is crucial as it is only when children are actively involved that they take responsibility for their learning.

NEGOTIATION

Boomer states that '. . .at best the children's learnings only approximate to the teacher's goals, so the curriculum may touch only a little of each child's key and associated interests.' (Boomer 1984, pp.122-3) It is clear that some negotiation of the curriculum is necessary if the learning is to be relevant to the needs and interests of the children. Andrea spends a great deal of time, especially at the beginning of the year, getting to know her class.

It is important to know each child as an individual: to get to know his/her interests at school and beyond. I rely heavily on this knowledge as it feeds my planning and is essential if learning is to be relevant and of interest.

While Andrea assumes responsibility for implementing a balanced program, she encourages the children to contribute to the curriculum. Her planning involves some negotiation with her students, and this occurs in various ways: by making suggestions, initiating research tasks, offering solutions to problems encountered in any given project and evaluating the effectiveness of resources. By planning and working this way the students are more likely to have a stake in their learning and it is more likely that the curriculum will build on what they already know and provide ways of exploring new information and skills.

FACTUAL TEXTS IN YEAR 6

In the past, class projects have been common in the upper year levels of primary school. Often this was the only time that children used factual texts. Factual writing and reading for class projects used a narrow range of often inappropriate textbooks and frequently resulted in the regurgitation of chunks of the textbooks with few clues as to the understanding achieved by the child and with little consideration of the way in which the project was written. These projects were often meaningless to the child and little ownership of the subject matter or of the writing occurred.

In Andrea's class the traditional class project has no place. Instead she uses factual texts in context, that is, in response to a need for information about a specific area of interest and in order to show how language is used for a given purpose. So that we can see how this occurs, let's look at a learning sequence about growing up in which a number of factual genres were highlighted.

A LEARNING SEQUENCE: GROWING UP

Overall Aim
To examine and contrast the features of growing up in the baby boomers period (1940s, 50s, and 60s) in which our parents grew up with those of our own childhoods.

Two Main Strands:

Subject area focus:
Social education

Social education aspects:

Focus questions
What are the features of growing up during the 1940s, 50s, and 60s?
What are the features of growing up during the 1980s and 90s?

Contributing questions
When (and where) were our parents born?
What was life like for our parents when they were growing up?
What affected their lives during their childhoods?
How does this compare with our lives?

Concepts: change, similarities, differences, technology

Literacy focus:
Review a range of factual text genres

Literacy aspects:

Focus questions
What is the most appropriate way to present findings?
(What is most appropriate for my purpose?)

Contributing questions
What is the purpose of a particular genre (such as recount, description, procedure, report, discussion, explanation, argument)?
How is it structured to meet its purpose?
When is this genre used in our society?
What examples can be found?

Social education dimensions:

Knowledge	*Skills*	*Values*	*Action*
Features of growing up vary according to many factors, such as generation, gender, education, technology	Interviewing Surveying Collating information Working as a group Determining own group focus	Growing up means different things to people. What we may see as important may not be to another person. Our values are influenced by many things, such as family, advertising, peers.	To investigate the childhoods of our parents. To highlight positive and negative aspects. To contrast with our childhoods.

Literacy dimensions:

Knowledge	*Skills*	*Values*	*Action*
A range of factual genres are available. The purpose determines the genre used	Identifying factual genres. Writing in various factual genres. Reading a range of factual genres. Selecting an appropriate genre for the task at hand.	It is useful to be able to read and write for a range of purposes. Using language in purposeful ways is enjoyable and enabling.	Using an appropriate factual genre for the given purpose or goal of using written language.

Figure 5.1 Overview of the 'growing up' unit

The unit grew out of a literature focus on fictional texts, such as *Playing Beattie Bow* and *The Green Wind*, which highlighted life in other times. After reading *Playing Beattie Bow* children made a list of important features of life in 1873 and compared them with the present.

Interest was sparked from this about what life was like when our parents were growing up. The students set off to ask their parents the year in which they were born. This then formed the basis of a class graph.

With such interest, Andrea planned her 'growing up' unit while keeping in mind her aim to review a number of factual genres before the end of the year. She developed the following learning sequence.

Confrontation activity:

A guest speaker talked about growing up in the 1950s.
Read *Baby Boomers*.

Concept development:

Individually each student listed words about the confrontation activity. These were then shared within a group of four or five and collated into a group list. The words were written on small cards and classified according to labels or headings decided on by the group.

The lists were shared as a whole class and collated on a wall display. As well as indicating the degree of concept development, the display acted as a resource for the whole class.

Wall displays act as a resource for the whole class.

Investigations:

A concept map was developed from the class list and formed the basis of topics to be investigated. The students chose an area of interest and formed groups accordingly. Each student listed three preferences which were handed to Andrea. She then tabulated interests and formed eight groups. The groups were centred around the following topics:

technology	advertising	games
American/English influence	jobs	food
fashion	transport	

Group contracts:

Before completing group contracts, Andrea showed the children how to generate questions about a given topic and how to find out the necessary information.

The groups discussed their topics and their main focus questions, and then each group submitted a contract to Andrea stating:
- what they wanted to find out
- how they intended to find out information
- what they needed in the way of help

For instance, the fashion group listed the following:

> We need to find out about: hair styles, clothes, teenage clothes, changes in clothes,
> We will survey our parents,
> We need to use the computer and the photocopier.

Gathering information:
Once each group had established its own focus and method of investigation, Andrea made sure that each group member was contributing. She checked contributions by close observation during group work, asking each student to record the tasks undertaken and discussing the allocation and completion of tasks in share time.

Many groups conducted surveys and spent much time planning their questions and then gathering the information. The fashion group wrote the following survey that was photocopied, distributed to parents and then collated. Other groups engaged in field work, consulted factual texts and magazines.

One of the fashion group members types up the survey on the classroom computer.

A MATTER OF FACT

Other groups engaged in field work.

Two group members gather information about cars from the staff car park.

EXPLICIT TEACHING

As the groups continued their investigations it became apparent that they needed to use various genres to suit their purposes. In order to review and to support the various writing needs of each group, Andrea revised a number of main factual genres during the course of the unit.

I demonstrated how to write a description by writing a description of Andrea with the help of her class. We listed the main features of Andrea and then added more detail. This data formed the basis of our description which was written as a whole class.

Then the students returned to their research groups. Each group was given an object to describe. The technology group described an old telephone from the 1950s (retrieved from the Prep play corner), the food group described a typical school lunch from the 1960s while the transport group, who had by this stage changed their focus to cars, described a Ford from the 1950s. They discussed the object in detail and then each student wrote a description using the format that I had demonstrated. One of the members of the games group wrote a description of a jar of marbles.

From this unit a number of factual genres emerged. For instance, the jobs/occupations group wrote a report about teachers from 'the olden days.'

LITERACY DEMANDS IN A YEAR 6 CLASS

Andrea and I developed a number of strategies to help students write in various genres.

LET'S WRITE A REPORT

A report tells about a group of things. It is different from a description as it is more general.

Author:

Topic of the report: _____

General items to report on:
(these will become your paragraphs)

1.
2.
3.
4.
5.

The Report:
(Remember that a report starts off in a general way. The first sentence tells us what the report is about in general.)

EXPLAIN THIS!

An explanation tells how something works.
Your first sentence must introduce the item that you are explaining.

LET'S HAVE AN ARGUMENT!

An argument gives reasons behind a statement that tells your point of view.

ISSUE: (what you are arguing about)

REASONS SUPPORTING YOUR ARGUMENT:

CONCLUSION

EXPLAIN THIS!

An explanation tells why something is the way it is
eg why people keep pets

Your first sentence must introduce the phenomenon that you are explaining.

LET'S WRITE A DESCRIPTION

A description is specific and tells what something is like.

Author: _____

Object: _____

Features	Reasons

Description:

WRITE A RECOUNT:

Recounts retell events that you have experienced. They often start with beginnings such as these:

I remember when I was ....

or

Last Saturday I ....

or

During the holidays ....

HOW TO _____

(Procedural writing tells how to do something.)

Author: _____

What you need:
(materials)

What to do:
(method or steps to follow)

WRITE A DISCUSSION

A discussion gives both sides of an argument.

ISSUE: (what you are arguing about)

ARGUMENT FOR:

ARGUMENT AGAINST:

CONCLUSION:

TIME WELL SPENT

Time was spent on gathering information: writing questions, exploring content through a range of sources and collating information. Because of this the students were confident about their content and were then free to concentrate on the genre of the writing that flowed from their group focus.

The groups discussed with us and among themselves an appropriate way of writing up their information. This overview of the topics and factual genres shows the variation that occurred.

Topic	Genre
TECHNOLOGY	Procedural
TRANSPORT (Cars)	Description
ADVERTISING	Description
GAMES	Recount
AMERICAN/ENGLISH INFLUENCE (focus on music)	Argument
JOBS	Report
FOOD	Report
FASHION	Report

Although the information had been gathered as a whole group effort, Andrea insisted that each student should write something. Individual students asked for help from us when needed.

The writing varied in complexity. Some students spent time revising their writing while others did not. Simon wrote a historical recount about soccer.

Soccer in the 50s, 60s and today. ~~Soccer~~ Popular Soccer Started in the late 1940's when the South Americans Started to get on top in the world by the early 50's when the Brazilians were the team of soccer, ~~they~~ produced some Skillful Players Such has Pele he was, Popular threw the 50s and 60's 60's he's last world cup was 1970 for Pele in Mexico City with a packed house, It was Brazil vs Italy.

LITERACY DEMANDS IN A YEAR 6 CLASS

One of the pieces of writing to emerge from the American/English influence group was an argument about music. This was the first time that the writer had used this genre independently.

LET'S HAVE AN ARGUMENT!

An argument gives reasons behind a statement that tells your point of view.

ISSUE: (what you are arguing about)
Rock music ~~tatatat~~ ~~kind~~ of m
and Whyy the music in the 60's and 50's is better
Roll than now

REASONS SUPPORTING YOUR ARGUMENT:
we think in the 50's and 60's Lyrics we better, crowds were bigger, and the slightest thing different was considered an outrage. the songs were slower and there wasn't any really heavy Guitar, and that appeals to a wider range of listeners. In the late sixty's folk music was big and alot was about vec how it bad meaning war was so that it's also very good. very soothing relaxing songs. expecially Bob Dylan,

CONCLUSION:
Why the music in the 60's and 50's is better than the music now.

- Difference was an outrage
- bigger crazier, crowds
- better ~~lyrics~~ meaningful lyrics
- slower.
- enjoyed by a wider range of people
- relaxing, soothing

'WHAT WE KNOW NOW' OR EVALUATION

The unit can be seen as a way of completing an overview of genres covered during the year, highlighting the students' options in reading and writing. Andrea constantly evaluated the unit during the regular group presentations of information and sharing of writing. The writing constructed at the end of the unit indicated what the students knew about their topics as well as their control of various factual genres.

Andrea also set aside time at the end of the unit for the students to reflect on their own learning.

One way of challenging the students to consider how they learnt took this form:

THINK ABOUT YOUR LEARNING!!!!!

HELPS	HINDERS
Teacher	time
Parents	fear
Friends	friends
Instructions	Teacher
eg.	Shy
pam	yourself
encouragment	interuption
time	When People but in T.V.
reading	
If you really want to do it.	
ask questions	
when people talk to you about it.	
School	

The reflections reveal the students' awareness of their own learning. They know a number of sources that help learning and are aware of the social nature of learning. The emphasis on talk, particularly asking questions, and the need to listen were common themes among the class.

LITERACY DEMANDS IN A YEAR 6 CLASS

Individual self-evaluations were completed. Learning more about social research was a success that many students mentioned. Many of the students wrote about a particular factual genre that they felt more competent in using.

SELF EVALUATION: NAME:

I learned how to *and* about research + looking up in book how 50's were different in the 40's 50's 60's

Things that helped me learn were... books... Pam, Miss Johnson, picture and information

I feel pleased about... the amount of work done, and how things have changed

Now I am an expert at... looking up things and put texts together

I feel concerned about... it... I did ~~enough~~ enough work on it.

I need to work on... surveys... and keeping the whole act, because when I opt the acts I cut out parts of it but later I found I need the other parts.

Next time I could try... a survey of some people opinion

READING AND WRITING OPTIONS

To conclude the unit we asked the students to list all the types of reading and writing which they were aware of. They wrote individually and then we collated a class list.

FICTION	Picture story books Choose your own adventure Fairy tales Riddles	Mystery Romance Comics Humorous Science fiction	Adventure Rhymes Horror Jokes Play scripts Novels
FACTUAL	Historical writing about the past (recounts) Cookbooks Biographies Debates Newspaper articles Explanations	How to's Diary (recount) Autobiographies Reviews (reports) Description Reports Arguments Magazine articles	

The above list shows the students' awareness of the uses of written language. They drew on their experiences with fictional texts as well as factual. They were keen to try to classify the list into two main groups. However, the discussion that accompanied such listing and classifying made it apparent that they were aware that some texts, such as diaries and biographies, overlapped this division. By providing a wealth of opportunities for her students to explore a wide range of texts, Andrea has helped to expand their reading and writing options.

6
CLASSROOM STRATEGIES

A LEARNING/TEACHING CYCLE

We can identify a learning/teaching cycle for exploring a new text genre from the three classrooms described.

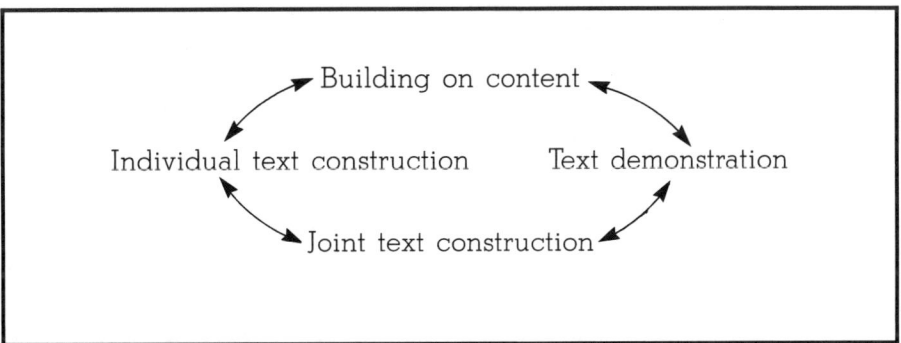

Figure 6.1 Learning/teaching cycle: extending text genre repertoires

BUILDING ON CONTENT

Although four main elements are depicted, the process is cyclical. For example, once individual text construction has occurred, the learning/teaching continues, perhaps by exploring another text genre or by revisiting and extending a known genre. This exploration can begin by building content or may start in text demonstration. The cycle can be entered at different points according to need.

When a new genre is introduced, its purpose, features and structure are made explicit in the text demonstration stage, where there is provision for talk and focused questioning about text. This usually occurs in the context of a shared experience, such as a science experiment or an excursion, although this may not necessarily represent the starting point.

It is important to build content knowledge (field) through a variety of shared experiences. For instance, when a Year 2/3 class decided to write a class cookbook, they spent time reading recipes, making shopping lists, buying ingredients, and cooking together before beginning to write. As they looked at the structure of procedural texts, they were also examining the organisation of the content.

Then the text *Let's Cook* was examined, explored and developed further and the appropriate genre (in this case procedural) was adopted.

In each of the three classrooms a large amount of time was provided for this aspect of the learning cycle. Each teacher stressed the importance of enabling students to feel confident and competent about the content. This made writing easier as the students were able to concentrate on the structure of their writing. The value of shared class knowledge was emphasised. By sharing experiences, such as whole class shared reading, group research and/or class excursions, the class had some common knowledge and experiences to talk about and to read and write about.

TEXT DEMONSTRATION (EXPLICIT TEACHING)

Although some of the terms used in the learning/teaching cycle are similar to those in the curriculum model developed by the Disadvantaged School Program in New South Wales, a number of differences are evident. (Callaghan and Rothery 1989, p.39) 'Modelling' is a much-used term, but it is not used in this cycle as it is associated with notions or implications of perfection. The notion of the teacher as a model is misleading as '. . .anyone who literally tries to model a skill performance after someone else will end up being mediocre at best. On the other hand, we do believe the examples are informing. Sometimes they provide glimpses of "miscalculations". Overall, they suggest a variety of ways in which it is possible to create a responsive and intelligent approach to reading instruction.' (Bussis, Chittenden, Amarel and Klausner 1985, p.198) Although Bussis et al. were referring to the teaching of reading, the same applies to the teaching of writing.

The term 'demonstration', which means the provision of an example with a view to providing information, is more appropriate. A demonstration may include 'miscalculations' or errors, which will also need to be made explicit to children via discussion. The demonstration can be extended further through group and/or individual application.

An example during the writing of a class recipe book was the teacher demonstrating on a chart one way of writing up a recipe. Later, each child used this structure as part of joint text construction.

Text demonstrations provide a guide for children's own text construction.

JOINT TEXT CONSTRUCTION

A range of activities are undertaken in preparation for the joint construction of a new text in the same genre. Joint construction of a text will usually be based on an authentic written text. Children jointly construct texts with adult partners. When a commercial text is used as an example, the joint text construction may result in what is actually an innovation on a text.

Joint negotiation of a text provides opportunity for what Boomer (1984) terms 'negotiating the curriculum'. This refers to '. . .deliberately planning to invite students to contribute to, and to modify, the educational program, so that they will have a real investment both in the learning journey and in the outcomes. Negotiation also means making explicit, and then confronting, the constraints of the learning context and the non-negotiable requirements that apply.' (Boomer 1984, p.125) Teaching within this cycle is planned and explicit, but the cycle is flexible enough to invite and give serious consideration to contributions by children.

INDIVIDUAL TEXT CONSTRUCTION

Once a child has experienced the authentic language demonstrations provided through repeated interaction and joint application, independent text construction may occur. In fact, the strategies employed in text demonstration and joint text negotiation encourage children to construct their own texts. A process of drafting, conferencing and consultation with teacher and peers, editing and revision of writing, may lead to polishing and then to publication. The photograph below shows Nita keying the results of individual text construction into the word processor at the publication stage of writing.

Nita keys in the text at the publication stage.

Some children relied more heavily on class books than commercial texts for ideas and structure in their own writing. For instance, Vulcan was reluctant initially to use the commercial texts by himself. He used the class charts generated from reading the commercial texts, the class texts and the accompanying writing experiences, which made the commercial texts more accessible. The children's publications provided examples and inspiration for each other as well as themselves.

Not all children will be ready to work independently at the same time and you may need to look at other examples of the particular genre being examined and jointly construct further texts before moving to the independent stage.

When writing independently, the child selects a genre to explore further, usually choosing from the range of genres that have been demonstrated to the class and from those which the class has explored jointly.

THE TEACHER'S ROLE

In the school setting, the teacher takes on many roles including that of instructor, which involves explicit teaching, and of facilitator, encouraging the learner to take responsibility for learning. A balance between these two roles can be achieved, and as the learning/teaching cycle above indicates, teaching is somewhere in between the two. The continuum between instruction and facilitation provides room for negotiation such as shared input, shared decision making and joint responsibility.

The role of the teacher incorporates:

INSTRUCTION ←	→ FACILITATION
explicit teaching	incidental teaching
teacher input	learner input
teacher demonstration	learner demonstration
(of knowledge/skills/values)	(of knowledge/skills/values)
teacher responsibility	learner responsibility
teacher decisions	learner decisions
teacher provision of resources	learner provision of resources
teacher text repertoire	learner text repertoire
teacher evaluation	learner evaluation

Within this continuum there are a multitude of tasks relating to planning, providing demonstrations of language in use for various purposes, displaying and making accessible appropriate resources as well as evaluating. For instance, we need to know when it is appropriate to provide explicit input and to insist that our planned activities are followed. At other times we need to allow students to make their own decisions about their learning.

A vital part of the teacher's role is being aware of and competent in using language for a range of purposes so that we can extend student's text repertoires. By knowing how to use language competently and by being familiar with a broad range of available texts, we are better able to provide the necessary scaffolds for language learning.

CLASSROOM DISCOURSE

The classroom discourse, or the talking and listening that is fostered in our classrooms, is vital to the learning that occurs. Schools have long emphasised written language over oral. As Heath (1986) noted, this tradition stems back to nineteenth-century schools. Much of the reading and writing that occurred served to keep large classes of children busy and under control. As a result little room existed for talk. Over the last decade or so there have been great changes in the frequency and kinds of talk that occurs in the classroom.

Research into classroom interaction has had great impact on what goes on in many schools. Tough (1979) pointed to the need for continual classroom interaction if the intentions and expectations of the teacher and the needs of the children are to be recognised. By talking *with* (rather than just *to* or *at*) children a teacher can begin to understand more about, and is better able to cater for, their individual learning needs. Such interaction enables children to convey needs, to play with language, to draw on their own experiences, to explore ideas beyond their own experiences, to think through ideas and to reflect on skills, with the support of the teacher and their peers.

WHO IS DOING THE TALKING?

According to Wells (1986), children '. . .don't learn only by listening. Since the motivation for learning language at all is to be able to communicate, children are constantly using the resources they have already acquired to interact with other people about their needs and interests and about the activities in which they are jointly engaged.' (Wells 1986, p.39) Children need opportunities to engage in meaningful talk. They learn by interacting with others. If the teacher is doing most of the talking, as Wells has found, then the children are probably spending most of their time listening (or tuning out). However, if the classroom invites talk, if transactions occur, rather than the transmission of information, learning is enhanced.

Hansen (1987) has highlighted the need for teachers to take time to listen. This means talking less and listening more, which opens up opportunity for children to talk, and to feel that what they are saying is valued.

IRE

We also need to evaluate our own talk, particularly the questions that we ask. The most commonly observed pattern of classroom interaction according to Cazden (1988) is I (initiation), R (response) and E (evaluation). The following exchange is an instance of IRE.

Teacher Did you enjoy the book?

Child: Yes.
Teacher: Good.

Furniss and Poulton (1991) consider ways of expanding this interaction to provide children with opportunities beyond one-word utterances. They encourage teachers to reflect on the classroom interaction that is occurring and to take action to use talk to its full potential as a support or scaffold for learning.

The teachers described in this book supported the discourse in their classrooms in various ways: by encouraging children to take part in whole class discussions and by gradually enabling them to take a greater role as the year progressed. Providing children with lists of possible questions to ask during conferences and informal talk about their reading and writing helps them to use the questions heard as a whole group and enables them to apply the questions when talking in whole group, small group and paired situations. These questions can be displayed in a prominent place in the room, as well as each child having an individual copy.

Palincsar and Brown's (1986) reciprocal teaching strategy structures both reading and talking about reading. This strategy involves adults and children taking turns to be the teacher. This strategy was adapted in Year 2/3 to act as a scaffold for talking about and reading factual texts. It was demonstrated by the teacher a number of times before the children could use it independently. When working independently a group of four children was formed and each child took a role, including predictor, questioner, summariser and clarifier. This strategy works well with factual texts that have clear headings and subheadings. Before a paragraph is read, the predictor encourages the group to guess what the text will be about. After the paragraph has been read, the questioner asks a question about the content. The summariser sums up the main content of the paragraph, and then the clarifier checks that everyone has understood the content before moving on to the next paragraph. This strategy provides a scaffold for talk as well as for reading.

A FEW QUESTIONS ABOUT CLASSROOM TALK

Some useful questions to consider:
- Who is doing the talking in the classroom?
- Who is doing the listening?
- What kinds of questions do I (the teacher) ask?
- What kinds of responses are generated?
- What does my questioning technique demonstrate to children about questioning?

- What kinds of questions do children ask?
- What opportunities exist for children to ask questions? or to talk about their work?
- How can I promote 'on task' or meaningful talk between a range of language users? (teacher/child, principal/child, child/child, child/parent-helper, child/cross-age partner)
- How can I use talk as a scaffold or support for learning?
- What will this mean in terms of grouping? scheduling? management?

As answers to some of these questions emerge, the vital place of talk in the classroom can be fully recognised and put into practice. This awareness has the potential to significantly alter the language learning that occurs in the primary classroom.

Providing for meaningful interaction is important to the children's oral language development and contributes to their reading and writing growth. The potential of such interaction must not be underestimated. Children can give each other support, ideas and motivation. Ideas of how to support one another also flow from teacher talk during introductory sessions, group conferences and share times.

LANGUAGE FOR LANGUAGE

If we are to examine language and communicate with others about language learning we need a metalanguage or language to 'talk' about language. A wide range of terminology emerged from the three classrooms. This broad range of terms:

- encourages students to be more explicit about their involvement in reading and writing;
- increases each student's repertoire of terms and their interest in words;
- provides students with appropriate terminology that others share and comprehend and so fosters meaningful interaction;
- expands each student's knowledge related to language use such as the roles in writing process, locational devices in texts, parts of speech, types of texts and text preferences.

A LIST OF TERMS

The terminology shown opposite was used in the three classrooms. The list is not exhaustive but may provide a useful starting point.

A SUPPORTIVE CLASSROOM: PROVIDING SCAFFOLDS

Teachers encourage learners to take 'risks' and to use language in a variety of ways. Learning can occur in a supportive environment, without the fear of being 'wrong', if mistakes are viewed as a natural part of learning. Learners learn through demonstrations of meaningful language by others and by using language for themselves. Decisions

CLASSROOM STRATEGIES

Roles within reading and writing
author
illustrator
editor
proofreader
publisher
printer
word processor
critical friend
reviewer
researcher
interviewer
writer
reader
listener
talker
questioner
predictor
clarifier
reporter
expert
authority

Parts of speech
verb (action word)
noun (naming word)
adjective (describing word)
conjunction (joining word)
pronoun
adverb
preposition
paragraph, essay
tenses (past, present, future)
word, phrase, clause, sentence
statement, question, exclamation

Other items
audience
message
meaning
conference
share time

Parts of a text
title, title page
heading, subheading
page, page number
copyright sign
chapter
chapter heading
print
illustration
photograph
diagram
label, caption
timeline
graph
table
figure
blurb
spine
cover
end papers

Punctuation
full stop
comma
apostrophe
question mark
talking marks
exclamation mark
brackets
colon
semicolon
capital letters

Textual elements
topic
fact
opinion
evidence
ideas
introduction
conclusion
points
beginning
ending
body of a text
recommendation

Types of texts
story
narrative
fictional
true
informative
factual
non-fiction
article
chart
book
letter
advertisement
newspaper
magazine
pamphlet
play script
debate
list
concept map

Locational devices
table of contents
index
glossary
heading
subheading

Factual genres
recount
description
procedure (how to)
report
explanation
argument
discussion
exposition

Text markers
bold print
italics
block letters
underline

made by learners are supported by a classroom environment which encourages and supports experimentation with language.

Such an environment helps to provide children with the scaffolds needed to support their language learning. The term 'scaffold' can be traced back to the work of Wood, Bruner and Ross (1976). The 'scaffolding' process is described as one that '. . .enables a child or novice to solve a problem, carry out a task, or achieve a goal which would be beyond his unassisted efforts.' (p.90)

The process is described under six main steps incorporating:
- recruiting the learner's interest in the problem at hand
- pitching the task at the learner's level
- keeping learners on task
- making critical features explicit
- avoiding over-dependency on the teacher while still offering support
- demonstrating or modelling the solutions to the task

(Wood, Bruner and Ross 1976, p.98)

CLASSROOM STRATEGIES

The notion of scaffolding is still applicable to the classroom. The structures that provided the most support in the three classrooms described may be seen to include:

> Predictable routines
> Choice
> Explicit teaching and jointly-constructed tasks
> Immersion in language and content
> Record-keeping

In order to provide maximum opportunities to use language in context, a wide range of strategies were used within each structure.

(a) PREDICTABLE ROUTINES

The importance of having a predictable class routine cannot be over emphasised. In an effort to find out how classroom routines were perceived by children, Year 2/3 children were asked to write an outline of what they would do if they were teaching writing. Nita's response is shown opposite.

The importance of predictable routines is clearly shown in Nita's writing. She has a clear idea of the classroom routine. She knows what the teacher's role usually entails and has clear expectations of this. She understands the importance of providing a clear text demonstration before independent writing. As well as being aware of a range of text genres, Nita has clearly indicated the main components of a writing session. Important aspects of this routine are the typical

> **4: I was the writing teacher**
>
> ① What I would do. I would tues a true book read it to the kids I would write an exemple before we read it ask the kids what sort of book it is When I have finished my exemple I would read the book then I would ask the kids to do what I done but dont copey myn. Then I would let the kids do there own writing I would help them and at the end we would have share time. I would want the kids to write true. books, Recounts, Miths, legends, Reports, Guessing books, when we have share time we would ask questions about the book.

components of the session, which include a whole class introduction involving explicit teaching, activity time into which individual and group conferences are incorporated and, finally, share time when the whole class joins together to celebrate achievements and share concerns.

A predictable routine supports the children because they know what is expected of them. It also means that they know when they can contribute to the class program. The predictable nature of the class routines in the three classrooms provided a scaffold for learning and included the following elements:

- Four components of sessions: introduction, focused text exploration, independent writing pursuits, share time;
- Daily writing, daily DEAR (drop everything and read) or USSR (uninterrupted sustained silent reading), both in regular time slots;
- Regular use of writing folders, first draft folders, have-a-go booklets, sound boxes/letter boxes (Clay 1985, p.65);
- Questioning in conferences and share time. In order to help my students to ask questions we generated a list of helpful questions. Copies of this list were kept in each child's writing folder:

A MATTER OF FACT

Let's have a conference.

Tell me about your piece of writing.

Where did you get the idea for your piece of writing

What part do you like best? Why?

Does your piece of writing make sense?

Do you have enough information?

Do you have too much information?

- Regular updating of writing topics and stages in the writing process (folders, teacher's book, class charts)
- Risk-taking (within a supportive environment)
- Constant expectations
  The wall banner displays an important class motto that enforces an important expectation: 'You'll never know if you don't have a go.'

Constant expectations provide a scaffold for learning.

- Use of experts (everyone has something to offer someone else);
- Feedback from others (roving conferences, group conferences, share time). Below, my Year 2/3 class share their procedural writing.

Regular feedback sessions provide support and encouragement, and opportunities to use language in context.

(b) CHOICE

Providing children with choices sustains their interest as they can make decisions about their learning and pursue tasks that they find meaningful. Opportunities for providing for choice include:
- seating arrangements (group or individual, access to materials, quiet corners)
- interaction with peers/teacher/other adults
- regular free choice/focused writing tasks
- options for conferences (small group, paired or individual)
- access to books, charts, other information sources
- publishing choices/decisions
- daily free-choice reading

(c) EXPLICIT TEACHING AND JOINTLY CONSTRUCTED TASKS

As well as providing for child choice, the program must include explicit teaching and jointly constructed tasks. Opportunities for exploring and developing various skills and understandings of the writing process and

the types of texts available for use are needed. The following activities may be used for explicit teaching and/or joint text construction:
- listing
- classifying (materials, text styles)
- labelling

Labelling activities develop writing skills.

- predicting from cover, title, format of texts
- summarising information
- forming questions about a text
- clarifying statements about a text
- isolating unique or special features of a text: format, layout, content, intended audience
- demonstrating writing for various purposes in varied styles including both fictional and factual texts
- demonstrating of proofreading, editing, publishing decisions
- demonstrating of lead sentences, titles, words that add impact
- displaying all information from text demonstrations on charts
- demonstrating, practising and displaying possible conference questions and techniques in pairs, whole class and small groups
- demonstrating the rewards of risk-taking, praising risk-takers
- demonstrating the existence of and the use of accessible experts (class peers, cross-age/older and younger children, teachers, principal, parents, siblings, authors, illustrators)

CLASSROOM STRATEGIES

Special features of a text can be isolated in explicit teaching sessions.

Information from text demonstrations is displayed on charts.

Children can use wide range of accessible experts.

- demonstrating and practising interview techniques and methods of recording information
- demonstrating publication options
- demonstrating selection of material to be published (critical judgements)
- varying groupings — individual, paired, small groups, whole class
- writing wall stories, story boards, story maps, story graphs
- writing a range of genres (narrative, such as poems, stories, myths, legends; factual such as recounts, descriptions, reports, procedures, explanations, arguments, discussions)
- using formats and specifics from demonstrated texts (such as tables of contents, blurbs, indexes, copyright, publishing details, glossaries)
- retelling information from another text
- gathering information from interviews, reading, reflection, discussion, observation
- recording and analysing information in point form, grid format, tables, graphs (bar, pie, cluster), maps
- comparing and classifying texts (fiction/factual; format, information, detail, audience, purpose)
- directed thinking activities, (such as retelling, summarising, co-operative cloze, directed illustration, sequencing, reciprocal teaching. (Palincsar and Brown, 1986)

CLASSROOM STRATEGIES

Is it a ten?

Title	1 2 3 4 5 6 7 8 9 10	Comments!
Skin Scales, Feathers and Fur	▨▨▨▨▨▨	I lernt that a shark has prickly scales all over its body
Lizards	▨▨▨▨▨▨▨▨	I didn't now that lizards could hide in tree holes but I do now
Animal Jig Saws	▨▨▨▨▨▨▨▨▨	I lernt that a cossaway eats humans
Mice mice mice	▨▨▨▨▨▨	I lernt about mice mice mice
An Alphabet of Australian Animals	▨▨▨▨▨▨▨▨▨▨	I lernt about all the Animals
Stone Soup		I lernt that it was an old Irish Tale
River red	▨▨▨▨▨▨	I lernt that a huge red gum tree grows from a tiny seed this big: ▯

- reviewing texts (example: is it a 10?)
- shared book readings

The effects of explicit teaching via demonstration and jointly constructed tasks can be seen in the children's understanding of various aspects and roles in the writing process. A few comments from my Year 2/3 children highlight this:

- **Locating information in a factual text:**

  You can use the table of contents. . . and what do you call it? It's at the back of the book. . . It's got page numbers and it tells you which. . . what you want. . . the index. . .

. . .table of contents. . . index. . . The table of contents tells you where it is and what page number it is on and the index tells you about it. You could look that up and say it's on page 15 or something. . . okay and then you could look in the glossary and it could tell you all about it and what it's got in it.

- **Editing:**

  . . .like fish, fish, fish books and we read it to them. And they [our year 5/6 cross age editors] check if it's right or not. If it makes sense.

  They [editors] tell us if it makes sense and they help us read it.

- **Revising:**

  Proofread it. . .you proofread it. To make sure it makes sense. We proofread because if the word isn't spelt properly. . . you could change it.

- **Publishing:**

  They [publishers] put the book together and put it in order and number the pages.

  Gets it ready and puts it in order and that to make sure that it's okay to publish.

(d) IMMERSION IN LANGUAGE AND IN CONTENT

By immersing children in both written and spoken language, an environment can be developed that motivates or encourages children to explore language in various ways, that demonstrates how language can be used, and that provides a resource or a number of reference points to act as scaffolds for their own language use. Children are also immersed in the content. Such immersion acts as an important scaffold for reading and writing. Some ideas to encourage this include:

Children's publications are prominently displayed.

- constant 'on task' talk (in context)
- inviting literature corners full of cushions, old comfortable chairs, and/or beanbags
- quiet work areas
- conferencing nooks
- displays of a range of texts (fiction and factual, in various forms including books, cards, magazines, pamphlets, newspapers, reference materials such as dictionaries, thesauruses, phone books and street directories)
- environmental print (labels, signs, directions)
- prominent display of new publications (from children, school and local libraries, bookclub membership)

The class post office encourages language use.

- displays of class publications (What's New?)
- display of children's 'special things' from home
- class post office
- class phone box
- class shop, weekly specials board
- class monthly newspaper

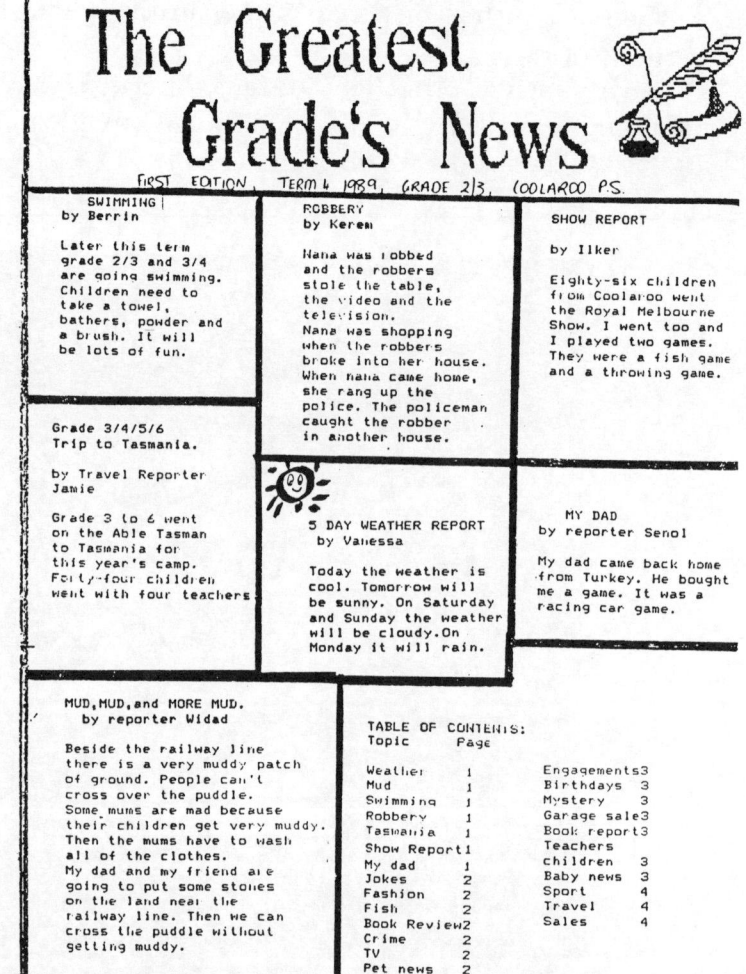

- class notice board of daily events (What's On?)
- graffiti board
- songs, poems, chants, rhymes, games, jokes, riddles
- drama, mime, role play, readers theatre
- time for exploration, rehearsal, informal play
- teacher use of appropriate terminology related to written texts (such as publish, author, editor, drafts, conference, table of contents, index, glossary, text genres)
- art responses

Children can respond through art-related activities.

(e) RECORD-KEEPING

As well as meeting the need to know *what* our children know and what they are pursuing in language, record-keeping can serve to inform us *how* children know what they know. By keeping continuous records and by including children in processes of assessment, both teachers and children can be better informed about their own learning and whether or not existing classroom programs and processes are meeting the needs of those involved. Such assessment can then shape the classroom program and involve children in their own learning, allowing them to take more responsibility for their learning.

The record-keeping used in the classrooms described in this book included:

- Planning diary or work program, units of work
- Reflective journal for teacher and children
- Writing folders:
  A manilla folder makes a useful writing folder. We stuck a plastic pocket in the centre to hold word lists, such as the 100 most common words, current drafts, conference question lists and have-a-go sheets.
- First draft folders:
  We used large art envelopes. These were labelled clearly with each child's name and kept in alphabetical order in a large box easily accessible to all.

Writing folder

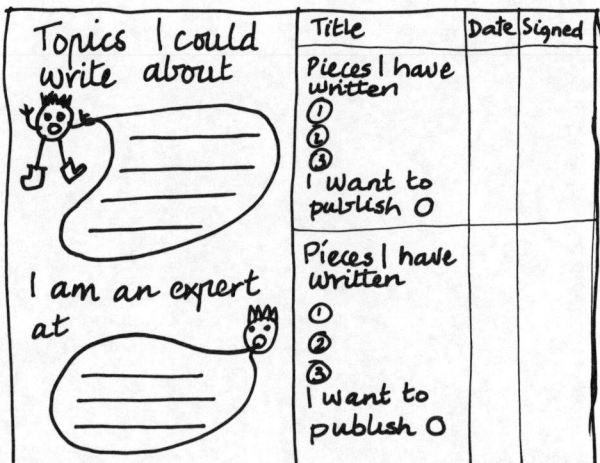

- Reading folders:
  Like the writing folder. The plastic pocket was useful for spare bookmarks, notes for related activities in progress and so on.

Reading Folder

- Reading reckoner:
  A pinboard can be used to record the borrowing of class made books. Label card pockets (often found in libraries) with the title of each class book can be used. Each child needs a name card which is kept in a spare large pocket when not in use.

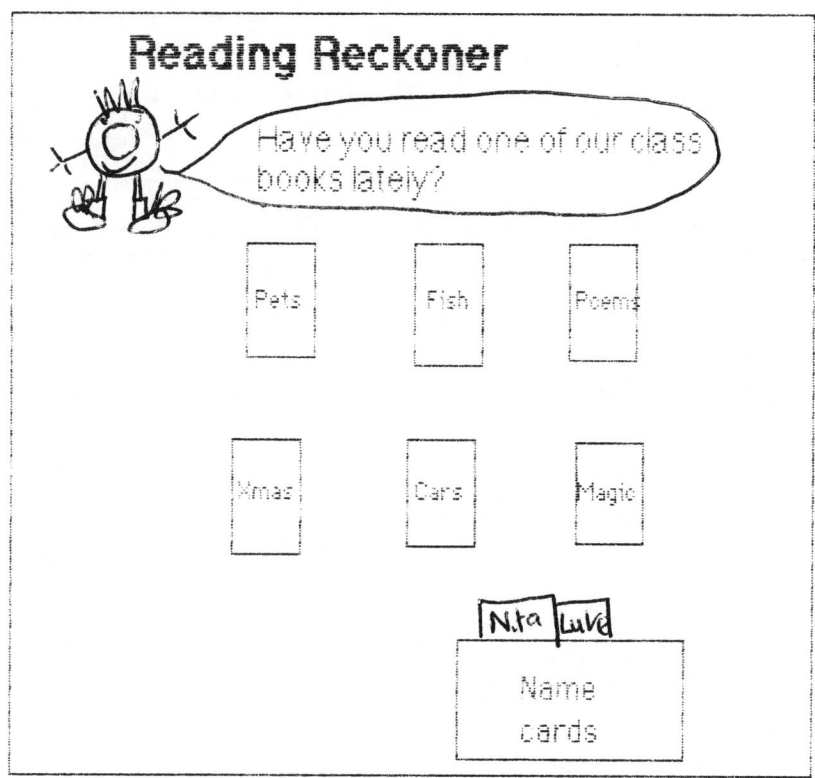

- Home borrowing book:
  If a dated record of home borrowing is needed, an exercise book or a folder or clip board containing individual record sheets for each child will suffice.

Name	Book title	Date borrowed	Date returned

- Have-a-go cards
- Teacher record book of conferences (individual and group):
  Use an exercise book to record conferences as they occur. Allow a

few pages for each child. Each time a conference takes place note the date, topic discussed and the next step as agreed upon.

Nita Year 3		
Date	Discussed	Action

- Independent writing task charts:
  A whiteboard in the class room is handy for keeping an up-to-date record:

Name	Title or topic	Writing stage
		(B = brainstorming W = writing P = publishing)

- Self-assessment sheets
- Class experts display:
  We created a class chart using the following format:

TERM 3
CLASS EXPERTS (or experts with class)

It is publicly announced that the following people have expert knowledge and skills:

Name	Expert Area
Nita	Spelling
Vulcan	Blurb
Luke	Indexes
Mick	Reports

This chart was updated regularly and it changed greatly over the year. At first the children wrote down content areas, particularly related to hobbies, as their expert areas. Every child indicated an expert area. Over the year additional areas of expertise were identified by the child and/or others. For instance, Luke identified golf as his expert area in February. By the end of the year he had the following added to his list of expertise: spelling, writing indexes, writing glossaries.

- Writing assessment over the year:
A useful way to record of each child's writing uses the following headings:

Month	Title or topic	Genre	Challenge

- Photography:
Taking photographs of successes over the year provides incentive as well as a valuable source of information.

Photographs celebrate successes and provide a valuable record.

7
GETTING STARTED OR EXPANDING OPTIONS

♦

There is a wealth of opportunities available to explore or extend various writing options, particularly factual genres, and a number of practical ideas are provided here. The ideas are broadly classified into eight main factual text genres. However, you may find that some of your writing pursuits cross over a number of genres blurring these distinctions. Most ideas could be adapted to suit any year level and could be pursued by individuals, pairs or small groups. Some of these ideas take the form of long-term projects while some are short term and others occur spontaneously as an opportunity arises from an unplanned moment.

RECOUNT
A recount refers to the retelling of past events. Let's recount some experiences. . .

- **Family history**

Children could interview one or two family members about how their family has celebrated important events over the years. They can write a history of their family's traditions and activities. (Include special foods, visitors, clothes, outings, rituals such as decorating a Christmas tree, gift making and giving.)

- **A holiday map**

Ask, does your family take holidays? If so, soak up recollections by

GETTING STARTED OR EXPANDING OPTIONS

perusing photograph albums or talking to family and friends. Children can construct a map depicting their family's travels, date each location and write a recount of a special family holiday.

- **I think that this year...**

Ask children to close their eyes and walk themselves back through the highlights and disappointments of last year. Then have them turn to the future and write a prediction about the year to come. Ask: Where will you be? Who will be with you? What will you do? What resolutions have you made? What will the year bring in terms of family and friends, pets, celebrations, holidays, weather, outings and the like? Have them keep this prediction and reflect upon it during the year. This could form the basis of an interesting diary entry.

- **A Year in the Life of _____ or 199- revisited**

Have children interview a friend about the important events during the school year and write a timeline from January to December, recording details of a few special events that their friend recounts. This could form the basis of a memento of the year and the class which could be presented in book form at a graduation or another end of year class function. This could be started early in the school year and updated regularly.

- **At times like this I feel . . .**

Have children brainstorm all of the feelings or emotions that a certain situation or experience brings. Situations might include unfortunate events such as accidents, losing something or having an argument with someone, or may include pleasant experiences such as special occasions like birthdays or Christmas. Have them classify these into groups and label them. Recount and record events that have occurred during the situation and match these to each emotion. Ask: What did you feel? What were the highlights? the lowlights? What range of emotions did you feel? Why? When?

- **Family journal**

Have children begin a journal for the whole class. They could record details of special events such as Book Week, achievements, visiting speakers, excursions, sporting activities and the like during the year.

- **Let's get into history**

Children could read a historical recount such as *Burke and Wills* and consider the way in which such recounts are worded and the details given about time, place and events. Have children write their own historical recount of an important part of history from their family background or an interesting aspect of Australian history such as the Ned Kelly gang. These recounts could form the basis of a historical journal or a series of informative books or articles.

PROCEDURAL TEXTS

A procedural text supplies details as to how something is done.

- **A class cookbook**

This project takes a little time but results in a keepsake of the year as well as a useful gift. *Let's Cook* and *Kids in the Kitchen* provide examples to work with when demonstrating to children how a cookbook works. The books contain locational devices such as a table of contents, an index and glossary that children might want to include in their own class cookbook.

- **Decorations**

Ask: Are you an expert at making a special decoration? If so, write out clear step-by-step instructions that might be useful to a friend who is wanting to make something new. Perhaps children could swap ideas by creating a Christmas decoration-making area in the room where such instructions could be displayed. This could be a great cross-age activity. (Some ideas: Christmas trees, paper stars, Christmas stockings, bells, chains, pomander balls, Christmas wreaths using a coat hanger, wire, green garbage bags, ribbon and tinsel, decorated soaps, bread dough decorations, marzipan figurines, papier mache masks). This can equally apply to Easter, sporting festivities and so on.

- **A board game**

Have children write the instructions for a board game. Perhaps they could base the game on the characters from a favourite picture storybook and put them into the book setting and related events.

- **Having a party?**

Have children write a party guide. They should include details about how to write an invitation; how to make your own special paper for the invitation (pin-pricked paper or marbled paper could make the invitation extra special. Refer to *Paper Crafts* for some great ways to make paper); how to plan a theme party; how to plan the party music; how to dance to the latest music; how to cater for a given number of guests; how to write a special menu; what to wear; how to play some new games as well as how to reply and what to take when invited to a party.

- **A treasure hunt**

Children could plan a treasure hunt in the school ground for the class. They should write signs indicating directions to take and provide class maps showing the pathway of the hunt. They could hide special (well-wrapped) treasures, such as homemade decorations, home cooking, cards, homemade puppets and the like which have been contributed by each participating class member.

- **199__ calendar**

Children make a calendar for next year. This could be a useful gift.

They should write in special birthdays, holidays, public holidays etc., and decorate with some of their writings, art work or photographs that they have created during the year.

- **End of year count down**

Children could draw up a calendar representing the remaining weeks of the year and the special events planned. This could take the form of a book, a huge chart in the shape of a Christmas tree, an advent calendar with special windows to open on a daily basis, or small charts each showing one week (each chart can be removed at the completion of the given week).

- **Post office**

Have children set up a post office for the whole school so that everyone corresponds with friends in the school. (At Christmas time letters from younger children could be forwarded to Santa.) This could be fun for Year 5 and 6 children to organise. They can write and display posters showing how the post office works. Details, such as delivery times, how to address an envelope clearly, how to design a stamp, ideas for making cards and the correct form of a letter to a friend, could be included. The local Post Office will have posters and stickers that will be useful.

- **Science**

Science experiments provide meaningful opportunities for procedural writing. For instance, if you are studying air pressure children could write the instructions for making a hot air balloon, listing what they need and then outlining the steps to be followed in order.

- **Magic**

Ask: Are you a budding magician? If so, share your talents by writing out some of your secrets in a how to do magic book or pamphlet. For example, children could write how to write and read invisible writing.

DESCRIPTION

A description tells what something is like. Usually specific in nature, a description might provide information about an individual person, animal, plant or object.

- **Mystery box**

Decorate a small box. Make sure that the lid can be removed easily so that the contents of the box can be changed regularly. Start the fun by placing a mystery object in the box and write a description for the class to read. Ask the children to guess the contents before you reveal the mystery. Hang your description in the room so that children can use it as an example for their own descriptions. Then the children in the class can take turns to take the box home and place a mystery item in it and bring it back to school on the following day with a description of the item. Class members read the description and make a guess. The descriptions could form the basis of a wall display or a class book or could be hung alongside each mystery object. (Alternatively, a small drawstring bag could be used.)

- **Vinegar herbs**

Have children dry a range of herbs from the garden and place in a bottle containing vinegar. They could decorate the top with a circle of colored material and a piece of ribbon, write a label describing the contents of the bottle, and describe uses for the particular herb vinegar that they have made.

- **'Garage' (classroom) sale**

Ask children to gather objects that they once treasured but now feel that they can do without. They can advertise a classroom sale by creating posters describing some of the objects on sale and the details regarding time and place. Perhaps they could write their own Trading Post and invite other classes to put up objects to sell. (The commission could contribute to an end of year party.)

- **Interview an author or two**

Have children talk to some authors within your class or beyond to discover tips for future writing. They should plan their questions and try them out on a friend. (Some ideas to get started with: Where do your ideas for writing come from? What do you do when you experience writer's block? How many drafts do you do? Where and when do you like to write? Who is a favourite author?) Have children write up their findings and describe each author and their writing habits.

- **Mystery seeds**

The class could engage in some gardening and so have plants to give as gifts by the end of the year. Bring a range of seeds (or seedlings or cuttings) and give each child the opportunity to bring along a container in which to plant them. Have children write a prediction for each planting in terms of what the plant might look like. They compare these predictions with the final results when the plants have grown.

- **Who am I?**

Read some books written in the inquiry format, such as *Hidden Animals* and *I Spy* for ideas about writing style and publication modes. Write the name of each class member on a card. Each class member selects a name and then writes a description of that person while keeping the identity of the person concealed. Children take turns to read and make guesses about each mystery classmate from the descriptions. This could form the basis of a class book which would serve as a reminder of classmates from the year. Photographs would add impact to the 'Who Am I?' book.

- **Peephole description**

Children select a photograph or magazine picture and write a description of the object or scene but do not reveal its identity. They cover the picture with card, leaving only a peephole revealing an interesting section, and display in the room alongside the description and invite others to guess the subject of the mystery picture.

REPORT

A report is more general than a description and provides details about a class or group of things.

- **An alphabet**

Children write an alphabet for a class book, chart or concertina fold book. Choose an appropriate theme, such as Australian animals or food, depending on your current focus. Provide information about each related object in general terms. You could use *An Alphabet of Australian Animals* as an example of report writing or as a basis for a text innovation.

- **Review the bookshelf**

Children read and discuss a range of picture storybooks, novels and/or some factual texts on a given topic of interest, and develop a range of criteria with which to judge the books. The librarian might be happy to be interviewed for ideas. Children write a report of recommendations for parents, class members and teachers who might find this useful in planning their own reading pursuits.

- **What do you eat?**

Children survey classmates and family about their daily eating habits. *What Did You Eat Today?* is a useful book to read for ideas about collating information into grids. Children may make a bar graph to show their findings. They could use their tabulated information to write a report about the nature of the food consumed by people. The report may form the basis of another piece of writing (an argument) explaining the need for a balanced diet and persuading people to reconsider their cooking pursuits and eating habits.

- **An excursion to the zoo (or a farm)**

If children have just been on an excursion to the zoo or a farm, they could try something different when they return to school rather than writing a recount of the event. Have children select an animal that most interested them and read some information about the animal. They may like to find a model from a zoo or farm set to observe closely. This may be useful in making a labelled sketch or diagram. They write a report about the animal in general terms covering aspects such as feeding habits, habitat including location on the globe (see if they can locate its natural habitat on a globe), movement and breeding.

- **Warning**

Children write a report warning people about the dangers of using chemicals within the home and/or at school. Consider chemicals such as those used in gardening, medical supplies, cleaning items and/or pool care. Find out what chemicals are most common and the potential dangers to health that are associated with them. This could lead to another kind of writing: procedural. They could write safety instructions for handling and storing such chemicals.

- **Keep in fashion**

Children survey the current fashions in the school yard and in newspapers and magazines, list the range of fashions found and match to the appropriate situation, age group, body shape, weather conditions and so on. They write a report about what is in fashion and what people are wearing.

ARGUMENT

An argument gives details as to why judgements are made.

- **Survival in the sun**

Children survey the school about ways of avoiding sunburn in the playground during summer and write up their findings with a plan of action to take to Junior School Council or School Council. Argue why such actions are needed. (Possible actions: mandatory wearing of hats, restricted outdoor play at 'dangerous' times of the day.) A pamphlet arguing for the need for being 'sunsmart' could be written and distributed within the school community.

- **A letter to Santa**

Children write a letter to Santa explaining why they might be deserving of a special gift that they have been dreaming about.

- **Debates**

Have a class debate. Children write their argument down in preparation. Issues could relate to any current affairs issue or to your integrated curriculum topic. For instance, when looking at the environment issues might include:
- the use of fossil fuels should be cut out completely
- on 'smog alert' days motorists should be required to share their cars or take public transport.

- **TV viewing**

Nothing to watch? Children review newspaper articles about television programming during the year and interview some classmates about their opinions of the options available at this time of the year. They could write a letter to a television station or to a local paper arguing why television viewing needs to be examined and that children ought to be consulted so that their interests are taken into account.

- **Elections for school council or class captain?**

If you are running for a position in the school you need to argue strongly why you should be the representative. This is where children will need to be able to write a convincing argument, listing all the reasons why they should be selected and sequencing them into a logical order. Children should write their argument beginning with a strong opening that makes it clear what they are writing about, argue their case by outlining what they offer to the position, and then conclude with a convincing statement recapping their strengths. This writing could form the basis of a speech and/or election pamphlets. Children could think of a catchy slogan to help their cause.

EXPLANATION

An explanation tells how something works or gives the reason(s) why some phenomenon is the way it is.

- **Why is it so?**

Do certain things surprise or intrigue you so that you find yourself asking 'Why is it so?' Children could make a list of things they want to investigate. They could read some factual texts about the topic — there are a number of books on the market that ask the question 'Why is it so?' — and use these to gather information and as the basis for their own text.

- **Why do people keep pets?**

Children talk to pet owners about the reasons for keeping pets. They should read some of the current literature about the benefits of keeping pets, such as the reduction of blood pressure and companionship and use the data to write an explanation of this widespread practice.

- **Why I am late for school**

Late again? Embarrassed? Have children write an explanation of their tardiness before they arrive at school. This may help to ease their embarrassment and explain in detail to the teacher why they are late.

- **How it works**

Ask children if they have ever wondered how a spider spins a web, how a CD works or how a telephone allows us to communicate with people in other parts of the world? A number of books answer the question 'How does it work?' Have children read these to discover some of the answers to their questions. Have them ask friends their most common questions about how things work and gather the information needed and present the answers in a weekly or monthly magazine about the wonders of nature or technology. They could invite others in the class to contribute feature articles.

DISCUSSION

A discussion provides both sides of an argument.

There are many opportunities for discussion. Encourage children to select an issue about which they know or for which they can find out about both sides of the related argument. Some issues may include:
- the land use at school
- the school tuck shop or canteen: healthy food issue
- the need for a school crossing
- the school rules

Such discussions may lead to action. Children may need to write to the school principal and/or the school council so that they take note of the issue. This could generate debate on the topic that they are concerned about.

EXPOSITION

An exposition takes a stance on a socially or scientifically significant issue. This is not common within the primary school as it involves sophisticated language use and also is a genre that is not frequently used by children in our society.

For instance, if the class is studying a significant issue such as the greenhouse effect, a number of possibilities arise. They could write an exposition on the topic such as:

> By the year 2020 the warming caused by the greenhouse effect will be so great that the polar regions will melt.
>
> The greenhouse effect will mean that. . .
>
> In order to reduce the impact of the greenhouse effect we need to. . .

AND FINALLY ...

- **A class newspaper (or magazine)**

Children could write a newspaper to distribute to parents and friends at various times during the year. You could use *The Southern Cross Herald* as an example of this kind of text. Perhaps an editing team could be organised to get the project off the ground. It would be wonderful if everyone could contribute an article. The newspaper could incorporate any of the above ideas, and more, thus using a range of text genres. In this way, you could communicate with the whole school community while demonstrating the writing repertoires of the entire class.

REFERENCES

Atwell, N. 1987, *In the middle: Writing, Reading and Learning with Adolescents,* Boynton/Cook, Upper Montclair, NJ.

Ashton-Warner, S. 1963, *Teacher,* Bantam Books, New York.

Bernstein, B. 1971, *Class, Codes and Control,* Routledge and Kegan Paul, London.

Bissex, G.L. 1980, *Gyns at Wrk: A Child Learns to Write and Read,* Harvard University Press, Cambridge, Massachusetts.

Boomer, G. 1984, 'Negotiating the curriculum', in Britton, J. (ed) *English Teaching: An International Exchange,* Heinemann, London.

Bean, W. and Bouffler, C. 1987, *Spell By Writing,* PETA, Rozelle, NSW.

Breakthrough to Literacy, 1970, School Councils Publications, Longman, London.

Britton, J. 1970, *Language and Learning,* University of Miami Press, Coral Gables, USA.

Brown, H. and Mathie, V. 1990, *Inside Whole Language: A Classroom View,* PETA, Rozelle, NSW.

Bussis, A.M., Chittenden, E.A., Amarel, M. and Klausner, E. 1985, *Inquiry Into Meaning: An Investigation of Learning To Read,* Lawrence Erlbaum, Hillsdale, NJ.

Butler, A. and Turbill, J. 1984, *Towards A Reading-Writing Classroom,* PETA, Rozelle, NSW.

Callaghan, M. and Rothery, J. 1989, *Teaching Factual Writing: A Genre Based Approach,* DSP Literacy Project Metropolitan East Region, Erskineville, NSW.

Calkins, L. 1983, *Lessons From A Child,* Heinemann, Portsmouth, NH.

Cambourne, B. 1984, 'Language, learning and literacy', in Butler, A. and Turbill, J. (eds) *Towards A Reading-Writing Classroom,* PETA, Rozelle, NSW.

Cambourne, B. 1988, *The Whole Story: Natural Learning and the Acquisition of Literacy in the Classroom,* Ashton-Scholastic, Auckland.

Cazden, C.B. 1988, *Classroom Discourse: The Language of Teaching and Learning,* Heinemann, Portsmouth, NH.

Chomsky, N. 1972, *Language and Mind,* Harcourt Brace Jovanovich, New York.

Christie, F. 1985, *Language Education,* Deakin University, Geelong.

Christie, F. 1987, 'Factual writing in the first years of school', in *Australian Journal of Reading,* ARA, vol. 10, no.4, November: 207-16.

Christie, F. (ed.) 1990, *Literacy for a Changing World,* ACER, Melbourne.

Christie, F., Martin, J. and Rothery, J. 1989, 'Genres make meaning; another reply to Sawyer and Watson', in *English in Australia,* no. 90, December: 43-59.

Clay, M. 1985, *The Early Detection of Reading Difficulties,* Heinemann, Auckland.

Clay, M. 1986, 'Young readers and their cultural connections', in *Australian Journal of Reading,* ARA, vol. 9, no. 4, November: 239-50.

Edelsky, C. 1991, *With Literacy and Justice for All: Rethinking the Social in Language and Education,* The Falmer Press, Hampshire.

Edmunds, F. 1979, *Rudolf Steiner Education: The Waldorf Schools,* Rudolf Steiner Press, London.

Enemburu, I.G. 1989, *Koori English,* Ministry of Education, Victoria.

Furniss, E. and Poulton, M. 1991, 'Classroom discourse', in Furniss, E. and Green, P. (eds) *The Literacy Agenda: Issues for the Nineties,* Eleanor Curtain, Melbourne.

Gee, J. 1990, *Social Linguistics and Literacies: Ideology in Discourses,* The Falmer Press, Hampshire.

Goddard, N. 1974, *Literacy: Language Experience Approaches,* Macmillan, London.

Goodman, K. 1986, *What's Whole in Whole Language?* Scholastic, Ontario.

Goodman, Y. 1978, 'Kid watching: an alternative to testing', in *National Elementary Principal,* vol. 57, no. 4, June: 41-5.

Green, P. 1991, *The Impact of a Range of Text Genres Upon Children's Writing: Implications for Classroom Practice,* Master of Education Thesis, La Trobe University, Bundoora, Victoria.

Green, P. and Green, M. 1991, 'Introducing factual texts: working with young children', in Furniss, E. and Green, P. (eds) *The Literacy Connection: Language and Learning across the Curriculum,* Eleanor Curtain, Melbourne.

Green, P. Leavold. S. McGregor. T. and McNamara, M. 1991, 'Who's talking now?' in *Classroom Discourse,* An intensive Course with Courtney Cazden, July, La Trobe University, Bundoora.

Halliday, M.A.K. 1981, 'Three aspects of children's language development: learning language, learning through language, learning about language', in Goodman, V.M. Haussler, M.M. and Strickland, D.S. *Oral and Written Language Development Research: Impact on the Schools,* IRA, Newark, USA: 7-22.

Halliday, M.A.K. and Hasan, R. 1985, *Language, Context and Text: Aspects of Language in a Social-Semiotic Perspective,* Deakin University, Geelong.

Hansen, J. 1987, *When Writers Read,* Heinemann, Portsmouth, NH.

Harrison, A. and McEvedy, M. 1987, *From Speech to Writing: Modelling, Evaluating and Negotiating Genres,* Robert Andersen, Melbourne.

Heath, S.B. 1983, *Ways with Words: Language, Life and Work in Communities and Classrooms,* Cambridge University Press, Cambridge.

REFERENCES

Heath, S.B. 1986, 'Literacy and language change', in Tannen, D., and Alatis, J. (eds) *Languages and Linguistics: The Interdependence of Theory, Data and Application,* Georgetown University Round Table on Languages and Linguistics, 1985, University Press, Washington DC.

Hill, S. and Hill, T. 1990, *The Collaborative Classroom,* Eleanor Curtain, Melbourne.

Holdaway, D. 1979, *The Foundations of Literacy,* Ashton-Scholastic, Gosford, NSW.

Hornsby, D. Sukarna, D. and Parry, J. 1986, *Read on: A Conference Approach to Reading,* Martin Education, Sydney.

Huck, C. 1989. *Children's Literature in the Elementary School,* Holt, Rinehart and Winston, New York.

Jaggar, A.M. 1989, 'Teacher as learner: implications for staff development', in Pinnell, G.S. and Matlin, M.L. (eds), *Teacher and Research: Language Learning in the Classroom,* IRA, Newark, DE.

Kantor, R.N., Anderson, T.H. and Armbruster, B.B. 1983, 'How inconsiderate are children's textbooks?' in *Journal of Curriculum Studies,* vol. 15, no. 1: 61-72.

Martin, J.R. 1985, *Factual Writing: Exploring and Challenging Social Reality,* Deakin University, Geelong.

Morris, B. 1989, 'Textbooks: Over-relied on but under-utilised', in *Australian Journal of Reading,* vol. 2. no. 4, November: 312-29

Ninio, A. and Bruner, J. 1978, 'The achievements and antecedents of labelling', in *Journal of Child Language,* vol. 5: 1-5.

O'Donohue, R.R. 1991, 'Why the Aboriginal child succeeds at the computer', in *Aboriginal Education Newsletter,* no. 6, ARA Special Interest Group in Aboriginal Education.

Palincsar, A.S. and Brown A.L. 1986, 'Interactive teaching to promote independent learning from text', in *The Reading Teacher,* vol. 39, no. 8. April: 771-7.

Parry, J. and Hornsby, D. 1985, *Write On: A Conference Approach to Writing,* Martin Education, Sydney.

Pigdon, K. and Woolley, M. 1989, 'Continuity and change: the development of holistic approaches to language and learning', in *Australian Journal of Reading,* vol. 102, no. 1, March: 57-61.

Rivalland, J. 1989, 'Meaningmaking: a juggling act', in *Australian Journal of Reading,* vol. 12, no. 1, March: 5-21.

Rosen, M. 1988, 'Will genre theory change the world?' in *English in Australia,* no. 86, December: 4-12.

Sawyer, W. and Watson, K. 1989, 'Further questions of genre', in *English in Australia,* no. 90, December: 27-41.

Scollon, R. and Scollon, S.B.K. 1981, *Narrative, Literacy and Face in Interethnic Communication,* Ablex, NJ.

Smith, F. 1983, 'Reading like a writer', in *Language Arts,* vol. 60, no. 5: 568-80, National Council of Teachers of English, Urbana, Illinois.

Tough, J. 1979, *Talk for Teaching and Learning,* Ward Lock Educational, London.

Walshe, R.D. 1981, *Every Child Can Write!* PETA, Rozelle, NSW.

Wells, G. 1986, *The Meaning Makers: Children Learning Language and Using Language,* Heinemann, Portsmouth, NH.

Wells, G. 1989, Foreword in Pinnell, G.S. and Matlin, M.L., *Teachers and Research: Language Learning in the Classroom,* IRA, Newark, DE.

Wood, D. Bruner, J. and Ross, G. 1976, 'The role of tutoring in problem solving', in *Journal of Child Psychology and Psychiatry,* vol. 17: 89-100

Children's books

Bingle, K. Bowden, D. and Dibley. 1990, *Your Backyard Jungle,* Harcourt Brace Jovanovich, Sydney.

Breidhal, H. 1989, *Bush Secrets,* Macmillan, Melbourne.

Caulfield North Central School. 1987, *Mice, Mice, Mice.* Macmillan, Melbourne.

Cowley, J. 1983, *Who Will Be My Mother?* Shortland Publications, Auckland.

Cullen, E. 1986, *An Introduction to Australian Spiders,* Martin Education, Sydney.

Drew, D. 1987, *Animal Clues,* Nelson, Melbourne

Drew, D. 1988, *What Did You Eat Today?* Nelson, Melbourne.

Drew, D. 1988, *Hidden Animals,* Nelson, Melbourne.

Drew, D. 1990, *I Spy,* Nelson, Melbourne.

Fowler, T. 1987, *The Green Wind,* Rigby, Melbourne.

Harvey, R. 1985, *Burke and Wills,* The Five Mile Press, Melbourne.

Klein, R. 1983, *Penny Pollard's Diary,* Oxford University Press, Melbourne.

Lancaster, J. 1989, *Paper Crafts,* Franklin Watts, London.

Leng, V. and Ryles, J. 1989, *Kids in the Kitchen,* Oxford University Press, Melbourne.

MacLeod, D. 1987, *The Southern Cross Herald,* Macmillan, Melbourne.

More Read it Again, Please, 1989, (An Anthology of Poems) Macmillan, Melbourne.

Neubecker, V. 1987, *An Alphabet of Australian Animals,* Macmillan, Melbourne.

Park, R. 1980, *Playing Beattie Bow,* Nelson, Melbourne.

Sydenham, S. 1989, *Let's Cook,* Macmillan, Melbourne.

Townsend, H. 1988, *Baby Boomers: Growing Up in Australia in the 1940s, 50s and 60s,* Simon and Schuster, Sydney.

Wignell, E. 1989, *What's Your Hobby?,* Macmillan, Melbourne.

INDEX

Aboriginal children 11
action 87, 130
assessment 61, 77, 79, 84, 106-8, 116-21 *see also* evaluation
audience 4, 27-31, 46, 68-80, 110

baby boomers 86-95
balanced program 34, 85
beginning school 34-57
blend of text genres *see* textual overlap
blurb 61, 64-5, 70
Boomer, G. 82, 85, 99-100
Breakthrough to Literacy 2

Callaghan, M. and Rothery, J. 10-12, 98
case studies
    Prep 34-57
    Year 2/3 58-80
    Nita 64-79
    Year 6 81-96
choice 3-4, 12, 54-55, 59, 62, 106-9
Christie, F. 6, 10, 12, 14
classroom discourse *see* oral language
classroom displays 35-38, 62-3, 88, 116-17
classroom layout 38, 63
classroom organisation 5, 18-19, 34-96
classroom resources 36-7, 62-3, 81, 85, 87-90, 100-1, 109-21
classroom strategies 97-121
community of learners, readers, writers 5, 36, 61-2, 80, 85, 98
concept map 88
concept development 48-52, 88
conceptual development (of texts) 28-30
conference approach 4-5
conferences 12, 59, 62-5, 80, 81-3, 100, 102-4, 108-9, 119-20

conference questions 18-19, 46, 103
'considerate' texts 28-30, 78
content (field) 5-6, 11-12, 16, 29, 49-56, 58, 64, 86-95, 97-8, 110
context *see* language as contextual
contracts 88-9
co-operative learning 52-4, 60, 81-92, 103
critical friend 80
culture *see* socio-cultural context

daily notice board 69-70, 116
data collection 70-5, 86-90, 112, 122-30
DEAR *see* USSR
demonstration 38-56, 59-80, 86-7, 90-1, 97-101, 106, 109-14
dialogue *see* interaction
diary writing 40-1, 68-9, 76-7
differences between fictional and factual texts 45-7
directed thinking activities 112

elaborated codes 1
empowerment 15-16
enabling 15-16
environment 37-8, 62-3, 106, 114-6
essayist society 13
evaluation 57, 94-6, 101-3, 116-21 *see also* assessment
expectations 34-5, 60-2, 81-3, 106-7
experts 60-2, 68-73, 109-10, 120-1
explicit teaching *see* demonstration

factual texts
    definition 20
    importance of 15-20
    selection criteria 28-32
    types of 21-8
feedback 4, 38, 85, 109
fictional texts 43-47, 96, 105
    see also genre: narrative, rhyme

first draft folders 117

genre
  approches 7-14
  argument 20-1, 23, 27, 86, 91-3, 96, 105, 112, 128-9
  classification (general/specific) 23
  definition 10-11
  description 25, 41, 57, 77, 79, 86, 91-2, 105, 112, 125-7
  discussion 20, 22-3, 28, 86, 91-2, 105, 112, 130
  explanation 20, 22-3, 28, 86, 91-2, 105, 112, 124-5
  exposition 20, 22-3, 105, 130
  main types 20-28
  narrative 66, 77, 79, 96, 105, 112
  procedural 20, 24, 48, 54, 57, 71, 77, 79, 86, 91-2, 96, 105, 112
  recount 20, 24, 57, 69, 77, 79, 86, 91-2, 96, 105, 112, 122-3
  report 20-1, 23, 26, 57, 72, 77, 79, 86, 91-2, 96, 105, 112, 127-8
  rhyme 67, 70, 77, 96, 105, 112
growing up 86-96

Halliday, M. 6-12
Hansel and Gretel 52-3
holistic approaches *see* whole language

ideology 11
illustrations, use of 30-2
immersion (in language and content) 5, 106, 114-16
individual/independent text construction 54, 59, 64-79, 92-3, 97, 100-1, 121
innovation on a text 73, 99
integrated curriculum 14, 16-17, 30-2, 127
interaction *see* oral language
inquiry 14, 16, 45-54, 58, 75-9, 126

joint text construction 51-4, 59, 68, 70-1, 77-9, 97, 99-100, 106, 109-14

kidwatchers 5
knowledge
  hierarchy 20,   22-3
  initial understandings 48-9
  general 29, 45, 86-7
  nature of 15, 20

language contextual 6-12
  functional 6-13
  'language experience' 2
  social 6-13
  system 6
  systemic functional model 6-13
learning
  conditions 5
  sequence 47-54, 86-96
  style 11
  teaching cycle 97-101
letter writing 41-2, 65, 128
links between home and school 2, 34-5
links between reading and writing 4-5, 19-20, 66-8, 70-1, 76-7, 80, 100-1
listening and speaking *see* oral language
locational devices 19-20, 29-32, 46, 51, 68, 71, 78-9, 105, 112-14

Martin, J. 12, 20, 23
meaning, kinds of 8-9, 12-13
metalanguage 13, 19, 104-5
modelling 98

Nauru 10-11
negotiation 85, 99-100
non-fiction 20

oral language
  classroom interaction transcripts 8-9, 43-5

forms 21-2
general 5, 12, 18-19, 34-5, 38-9, 42-6, 60-1, 73, 76, 82, 95, 102-5
genres 10, 21-2, 34-5
IRE 102-3
terminology 18-19, 30-1, 51, 104-5, 116
tradition 10-11

parts of speech 105
phonics 2
photographs, use of 17, 30-2, 127
play 2, 55, 116
predictable routines 59, 82, 106-8
process 3-7
product 7
projects 86
proof reading 9, 51, 60, 70, 73, 110
publication *see* writing
punctuation 78, 105

questioning *see* conference questions

reading
  connections with writing 4-5, 19-20, 66-8, 70-1, 76-7, 80, 100-1
  cue systems 45
  early reading 2, 34-5, 42-7
  folder 118

home borrowing 119
like a writer 4-5, 19-20, 66-8, 70-1, 76-7, 80, 100-1
prediction 42-7, 74-5, 110
purposes for 16-17, 20-3
  reckoner 119
  roles 105
  shared book 17, 42-6
  USSR 17, 45, 47, 55-6, 60, 107
reciprocal teaching 103, 112
reflection 14, 82-3, 94-5
register 11-12
repertoires 17-18, 66, 73, 76, 78, 95-7, 101, 104, 130
responsibility 3, 81-2, 101
restricted codes 1-2
risk taking 5, 34-5, 61-2, 104, 106, 108, 110
Roadville 11

scaffolding 35, 82, 104, 106, 114
share time 18, 37, 59-61, 104
shopping unit 47, 54
skills 87, 109-14
social education *see* units
sociocultural context 10-12
sound boxes/letter boxes 72-3, 107
speaking and listening *see* oral language
spelling 3-4, 70-3, 78-9, 107